GETTING ANSWERS

※

If you've picked up this book,
you are looking for answers—
and now you are also aware
that you can get those answers.

— Aimée

✳

GETTING ANSWERS

Using Your Intuition
to Discover Your Best Life

By AIMÉE COLETTE CARTIER

Spreading Blessings Media
Vashon, WA

Comments and inquiries regarding this book may be sent
to the author at www.spreadingblessings.com.

ISBN-10: 0982788401
ISBN-13: 9780982788400

Published by:
Spreading Blessings Media
PO Box 2332 Vashon, WA 98070

Book Layout and Design:
Tracy Barrett

Cover Art:
Jacqui Lown

Back Cover Photo:
Kirsten Szykitka

The passage reprinted with permission on page 20 of this book is from Ranier Maria
Rilke, *Letters to a Young Poet*, translated by Stephen Mitchell, (Random House, 1984).

More information about Aimée Cartier and her work can be found at
www.spreadingblessings.com.

Aimée Cartier is available for readings and speaking engagements through
www.spreadingblessings.com or contact@spreadingblessings.com.

This book is available through your local bookstore and www.amazon.com, and
barnesandnoble.com.

You may also order it directly by contacting us at www.spreadingblessings.com.

Contents

Foreword

This is a book about living an awakened life. For whole stretches of our lives we can live feeling as if life is thrust upon us—the good and the bad, the wanted and the unwanted. Then, at some stage, we awaken. Some of us awaken with a hope, a wish for a life that is greater, sweeter, more fulfilling. Some of us awaken into a crisis where we are forced to let go of something, or hold onto something, we never imagined we could. If you relate to this, if you're longing for a life that is freer or more in tune with your deepest Truth, if you're at some kind of crossroads, this book is for you.

Over the course of going through *Getting Answers*, you'll have the privilege to spend time with Aimée Cartier. A couple of years ago I called Aimée from New York in a panic. "Aimée, I've lost the keys to my friend's minivan. Can you tell me where they are?" She chuckled sweetly, "Sorry Babe, you're on your own with this one. I'm not that kind of psychic. But I'm sure you'll be fine." I was fine. I never found the keys but we worked something else out. And I learned that Aimée is not that kind of psychic.

I've known Aimée for the better part of 10 years now and have come to rely on her for her unique guidance as well as her friendship. As someone who works with the hearts and lives of people, I was so happy to hear that she was publishing a book. Aimée is gifted with a vision for things that take place beneath the surface of life. She can see currents and depths that are beyond the reach of most people because we're too busy to slow down and tune in. In ancient times, Aimée would have been our tribal shaman or an oracle, a source for answers. In this life, she has chosen so generously to clue us in on how we ourselves can feel the currents shifting, how we can get our own answers. In a conversational, easy-on-the-eyes way, *Getting Answers*, lays out an approach to conscious living that empowers us to be deeply guided from within ourselves and to be simply happy.

As an intuitive, Aimée is the "real deal." She is one of the deepest people I know, but as you'll see in this book, her guidance is not esoteric. It's profound, but it's not exotic. *Getting Answers*, is the sort of life tool that one day—perhaps a day not too far from this one—mothers and fathers will pass on to their children.

Getting Answers, isn't a technique or a gimmick for tapping into psychic powers. Rather it is an approach to life, a way of living with our eyes wide open to the guidance that is all around us. As Aimée suggests,

> Don't try too hard to find your answers. Trust me, it's easy. Especially once you've broadened your awareness to realize that anything could actually be an answer, Spirit will make it obvious for you.

In this book, Aimée's crystal clear goal is to empower each of us to become more alive and awake within our life. Living this way, our time on earth together becomes like a celebration hall waiting for our decorations and dancing.

Chances are you've picked up this book at an important time. The right time. Read on, and let the dancing begin.

Harshada Wagner
meditation teacher and founder of Living Meditation
http://livingmeditation.org

Introduction

It was my grandfather who first taught me that life is fun and it's meant to be enjoyed. It's not that he ever said those words specifically. He didn't sit me down on the porch and say, "Aimée pay attention: Life is fun." It was simply what he did. To Gramps, no subject was sacred from a bout of giggles. Whether he was making fun of you or you were making fun of him, the joy was the same.

I have beautiful and exquisite memories of laughing to the point of peeing my pants over jokes my grandfather told. Not because the jokes were funny, but because he would get to laughing so hard that you just couldn't help yourself. Sitting in proximity to his guffaws set you on a course to touch your own joy. It was contagious.

My grandfather's laughter was one of the most prominent aspects of what seemed to be his primary motto: Life is a game. The other outstanding feature of his attitude was exhibited in his eyes. More often than not they held a special sparkle. When you looked into them, you had the feeling he knew something you didn't. It wasn't a secret he was purposely keeping from you. It was just a joke so obvious and delightful that it shone through his eyes almost without his trying. I had the sense that even he couldn't quite define it—and yet it was crucial.

I was thinking of my grandfather recently while I was on a walk. I was reveling in amazement at the arrival of yet another answer to another of the burning questions of my life when I thought, *So this is what Gramps meant! This is precisely what that sparkle in his eyes always said: "It's fun. It's easy. It's a game. You'll see."*

Just like I did, you are about to discover what my grandfather knew. It's the simplest and most delightful game you may ever play. Why? Because it gets you exactly what you want—the answers to the questions of your life. The game never gets old because not only do your questions always change, but the ways in which you receive answers can vary so much, it feels like continuously discovering rich and magical surprises.

And as I said, it's easy! To me, identifying the process of *Getting Answers*, has felt simultaneously like discovering a great and hidden key, being the brunt of a huge joke (because it's just so darned simple) and opening a storehouse of joy incredible beyond imagining. My discoveries have been awe-inspiring, hilarious, deeply moving, startling, peaceful, and just plain fun.

At the heart of it all, you are in a dialogue with Great Spirit. Call this whatever you like, God, Goddess, the Divine, Spirit, Great Mother, Highest Self, Universe (all terms that I may use). In this Getting Answers process you get in touch with a deeply moving and expansive relationship with something so much larger than yourself that you can't help but laugh at your own smallness. And yet the more you play, the more you discover this absolutely amazing thing—the Universe is listening to you. It wants to give you the answers to your most burning questions. It wants you to understand—yourself, or your next steps, or how to save money, or what this relationship means, or what you are really looking for… whatever it is that you want to know. In fact, it's just waiting for you to ask.

It's this asking—this natural urge to find new ways to live or do things—that to me symbolizes the very essence of life. The same mysterious force and urge that causes a seed to transform into a flower, also rules each of us. Essentially, it is a desire to evolve and grow. Naturally, the Universe conspires to make it so. You can see this very clearly in children. They're always striving to attain the next level—be it riding a bike without training wheels, tying their own shoes, learning to read, or even mastering a board game. Children have an unrestrained and almost unquenchable thirst to become something more. We tend to forget this, but as adults, we are no different. Our quests come in different ways—an increased salary, a promotion at work, a new partnership, expanded creativity. Whatever we are searching for, longing for, or endeavoring to create is a natural expression of the fundamental urge of life to expand and create again anew. Our questioning comes from an innate need to evolve, to change, to grow, to thrive, and to experience more than we have before. This is life.

As an intuitive, many of the questions that I hear from my clients every day (and experience myself) arise from that innate urge to evolve. Questions like this: *How can I make more money? What are my next steps? How can I find a job that I love with health benefits?* This fundamental impulse to expand expresses itself in the practicalities of our lives. Whether we realize it or not, we reach for change, we need it, to live, we must have it.

The other type of questions that I hear from my clients (and experience myself) come from what I see as a hunger in each of us to do what is best, our natural drive to thrive. We want to know the best way to handle the situations life presents us. We ask questions: *What is the best school for my child? Where is the best place for me to live? What should I do about this relationship?* We endeavor to choose the answers that are best for ourselves and for those that we love.

The questions that we have in life set our direction; they either steer us on a course for our own evolution or they endeavor to make the most of what we are given. In both cases these questions, and the ways in which we choose to answer them, actually weave the very fabric of our lives. Our choices create results, which produce other experiences, other circumstances, and eventually other sets of questions.

This book details the method I use to get the answers to the questions of my own life. At its heart, this method gives the most basic formula of how a seer like myself gets answers. It is a way of looking that comes naturally to me. The older I've gotten, the more aware I've become of it, and the more fine-tuned I've become in understanding the ways in which this process works. However, it's exactly the same procedure I've used for years, even when I wasn't aware of the specific steps. It's the process that has, time and time again, allowed me to follow the lead of Spirit, express this natural urge to thrive, and to easefully walk my way into the most extraordinary beauty and magic that this human life offers.

This book gives the simplest and most effective technique I know of finding the answers to the very personal questions that riddle you and your life. It's as easy as it could possibly be, but it is, as you will discover, unfailingly marvelous in its effect. I have used it to understand what I am really looking for, as well as to get really practical information on how to handle a situation or what to do next.

The more questions you ask, the more answers you get. These answers in turn lead you to more questions. For example, if you don't know exactly what you are looking for, you can ask that very question. Once you find out what you're looking for, you might then want to know how to get it. Each question leads you not only to an answer, but also often, to the next question. In this way, the process becomes like a continuously changing and very exciting game. As you go along, driven by that natural urge for life, you realize there is always something new you want to know, there is always another answer you can have. By playing this game, you enter into what amounts to a continuous dialogue with Spirit, with the answers and results emerging on the canvas of your life.

What I've discovered is that asking the right question can and does change my life. One question always leads to another, and you can have the answer to any question you want to ask. It's that simple.

It is my hope that this book will guide you in discovering the most simple, fun, and satisfying way that I know of answering the questions of your life. In my experience it is the way that also guides you into the best and most beautiful life for yourself. In the process, I hope you will relish the experience, revel in its magic, and fully learn what my grandfather always seemed to know—it is fun *and* it's easy. You'll see.

CHAPTER 1

Align with the Highest Good

The decisions that we make literally weave and create the very fabric of our lives. What we choose to do, how we choose to respond, where we choose to go—any of this can have dramatic results. To go left or right in one specific moment can sometimes radically alter the course of our lives.

When I was in my twenties, I made a series of decisions that ended up entirely reshaping the way I live, in a fundamental way. These decisions, and more importantly their results, literally transformed how I operated and how I went about making choices from then on. Ironically, it was a series of "wrong" choices that taught me how to make "right" decisions. First, I chose to move across the country when I knew it was not the best thing for me to do. Later, I chose to date someone my intuition told me not to get involved with. Although my instincts clearly indicated that I should avoid both of these scenarios, because I couldn't see the reason for it, I overruled my own intuition. Suffice it to say, in both cases I found out eventually why these situations would have been better avoided. Two words could best sum up the whole experience: *drama* and *trauma*.

Looking back, though, I don't regret it. I mean, sure it would have been easier—much easier and much better—if I hadn't made those choices. However, living through and watching the consequences of those actions lead me very directly to the way I make decisions now. One, I gave up overruling my intuition. Two, eventually it caused me to recognize the process that guided me to the best results. That is the subject of this book: *Getting Answers*. Since that time in making every major decision (and most small ones) I have been guided by the process I am about to teach you. Even before I became conscious of the four simple steps of this process, I was applying them.

Following that course has led me so many places. For sure it has led me to my life as a professional intuitive, writer, teacher, and speaker. But also in hundreds, maybe thousands, of instances it has lead me straight to the path of joy—more joy than I could have ever conceived of myself. It has brought me homes, animals, encouragement, meaningful moments, profound connections, deep friendships and freeing experiences just to name a few. And possibly, although you've probably already learned from a few of your own mistakes, it will also lead you to the easy joy that is waiting for you. I would love to help you discover, sooner, and with less drama than I did—that Spirit constantly guides you, and provides you with clues that lead you to your best life. If you pay attention to these clues, and follow their guidance, you can begin to move immediately in the directions that create your best life.

Looking back on that time period in my twenties, what remains prominent in my memory is the untold number of circumstances where Spirit was giving me answers. In many of the same ways that I detail in the chapter on receiving answers, I see that at every turn the Universe was trying to get me to correct course. However, at that time, I also didn't know what I'm going to teach you about fear, so instead of correcting immediately, it took me months to finally act on the advice that the Universe had been giving me. Thankfully, the results were instantaneous and gratifying. The doom and gloom lifted from my spirit and I sailed almost instantly back into harmony with my own soul in a way that I hadn't been when I was ruled by those poor choices. I never forgot that lesson. It has shaped my life ever since.

Eleanor Roosevelt said, "Learn from the mistakes of others. You can't live long enough to make them all yourself." That's good advice. If you are off course, I'm going to teach you how to get back on; if you are on course, I'm going to teach you how to make it even easier. The first step to doing this is to align with the greatest good.

The truth is that there are a lot of possible solutions to any given problem. If you're looking for a way to get more money for example, you could rob a gas station. It's true. You could. You could also hold up the next person you see with that fake-gun-in-your-pocket trick we always see in the movies. That could work too. It could get you more money—at least for a moment. There are actually thousands of solutions to any given problem or issue, but you're not looking for just any solution. I mean truly, unless your bigger goal is to spend some time in jail, the first two options mentioned here are not your best ways of acquiring wealth.

The first step in getting your best answers is setting your radar so that you are only tuned in to the solutions that serve your best interest. These are the answers that in turn also serve the world. When you're aligned with this greater good, you do not receive answers that are good for you but harm others. You will not hear, for example, "Duct tape your husband's mouth shut," as a solution to solving disagreements between the two of you. You may hear, "Write him a letter," or "Read this book," but you will not receive answers that are not beneficial for either you or the others involved.

One of my teachers once said, "So your intention, so your attainment." Think about this. It is very simple. So your intention, so your attainment. Period. There isn't a single caveat in that whole statement; it's very specific. Intention equals results. Probably because the statement was so specific and simple, from the first time I heard it, it was burned into my memory. Not long ago I got to see the proof in action. I was flipping through some old notebooks, looking for a poem I hoped I had recorded during a certain time in my life. Although I didn't find the poem, I discovered something else that astounded me.

At the time of writing that journal, I had just quit my job and was figuring out what to do next. I felt extremely lost. I knew that I didn't want to be doing what I had been doing, but I wasn't really sure what I wanted to do. I began by brainstorming. I wrote down all of the ideas of the best and most rewarding things I could envision for myself. I listed specific qualities. When I had the best, I wrote them out into intention statements. I wrote things like, "I am an independent consultant. I am paid generously. My writing leads me to more interesting ideas and people who contribute to my growth. I live in a beautiful house that shelters, nourishes, and inspires me." I even had a list of specifics like, "I interview psychics. I have the ability to work from home or wherever I chose. I inspire myself and others to live up to our true potential."

Let me tell you, when I wrote this list I felt very far from achieving it. At the time almost every single one of the things I listed seemed like to total pipe dream. But I remembered what my teacher said about intention, and I held onto that. Now, many years later, as I was reading through that journal, I felt shocked in realizing that every single one of these things had come true. Within a year of my writing those statements I was offered job as a consultant for Conscious One, an internet company specializing in personal growth that provides online courses offered by many of the worlds leading spiritual and personal growth teachers. I was interviewing other psychics and interacting with some well-known self-growth experts of our time! All of the articles I wrote were, in one way or another, about living up to your true potential. I worked from home. I had found and was living in a gorgeous home that inspired and nourished me daily with its beauty. Every single one of the things that I had put on my list had come true. And, almost every single one of those things had found me. I was offered that job while I was taking a Conscious One course! With the house, a man actually knocked on my door one day and said, "I heard you were looking for a place to live. You should see this house I've got for rent." (No kidding.) Within a month I'd moved in.

This is the magic of intention. What you intend is what you get—even if you don't know how to get there. So take it seriously. When you start out looking for answers, you want to take the time to align with the greatest good. You want to set your intention so that you are only receiving information and answers that are in line with what is truly the best. This is what brings you the most rewarding solutions.

State your intention

How do you do this? Well, one way is to say a statement aloud. Before you ask a question, say something like this: *I receive only answers that are in line with my highest good.* Until it becomes second nature for you and you have enough practice to know that you are tuned in only to that frequency, you will want to reaffirm a statement like this every time you ask a question. You can find a way to say it that is most comfortable to you, using whatever words most resonate with your life. The statement will act as a reminder to the Universe that these are the types of solutions you are looking for. Not just any old answer to your problem will do' you want what's best for you and the world at this time.

One of the loveliest things about this whole process is how fine-tuned it is. When you ask questions, you will receive answers that are perfect for you right now. We are not talking about a generic self-help article list of things to consider (although don't get me wrong, those can provide great solutions) nor the response that would be right for your neighbor, or your mother. We're talking about specific solutions for you, Betty-Want-Some-Answers, or me, Aimée Colette Cartier, right now.

Not too long ago I was ending a relationship. My boyfriend of a year and a half and I had decided to split up. During most of the time we were together, he had been supporting both of us. So when it came time for the break up, it was obvious that I needed an income and fast! I applied for a job at a flower shop and as a waitress.

I got both jobs. My goal was to take the pressure off of my own business of writing and doing intuitive readings so that I could grow them each naturally and without stress. I kept all of my clients and continued to both write and do readings as well as hold down these two part-time jobs. Several months down the line however, I was exhausted. I felt as though my every moment was spoken for. When I wasn't at the flower shop, I was keeping up with the demands of my writing clients and my own business blogs and daily blessings. I was still doing readings and was going into the city several times a week to see intuitive clients there. On top of that, things at the flower shop were not going well. Contrary to what you might think it was actually a dreary place to work. The floral designer was constantly complaining, and the owner had such particular needs that no one but himself could ever satisfy them. Instead of hearing a "Thanks for dusting the store," I would hear a "Oh, you missed a spot." Day in and day out this was the case. After a while I started to dread going to work.

When this happened it became obvious that I needed to leave the flower shop. Except for the income it provided, the job was no longer serving me in any way. I was miserable the whole time I was there. I felt disempowered by the constant criticism and drained from listening to the non-stop complaining. Still I stayed.

A month later when my friends started asking me why I was still there, I had to start asking myself questions: *What's keeping me from leaving the flower shop? When I know I have to leave, why haven't I left?* The answer was obvious. Fear. I was afraid that leaving the flower shop would cause me a lot of financial stress. I felt so committed to creating ease in my life around the area of finances that my leaving a steady and regular, albeit misery-producing income felt like a huge setback to me. Even though I could clearly see the amount of pain and stress that this measly little flower shop job added to my life, and could recognize that my presence there contributed little toward what I was really here to do, I couldn't bring myself to break the cycle because I was afraid of the consequences to my financial well-being.

I was pondering this one day when I landed on what the real question for me was at that time: *How can I leave the flower shop gracefully, easefully, and without regret?* Once I acknowledged this to myself, I felt a surge of peace inside. It was like the universe had been waiting for me to ask that question. I wrote it out in my journal, making the letters bold and black. I realized that this is what I really wanted to know.

It was Sunday night.

On Monday morning I opened my email inbox and saw a message from someone I had never met before.

"Hi, My name is Stephen Silha," the message went. "I'm starting something called the Big Joy Project. It's a documentary film on the life and work of poet and filmmaker James Broughton. I'm looking for someone to help me part-time. You were recommended to me, and I wondered if you might be interested in meeting to discuss the project."

Yes I was! A few days later, we met. I told him what I charged for this type of work (triple what I was making at the flower shop). He said that was within his budget and shortly after our collaboration began.

Still, it took a leap of faith for me to quit the flower shop, which I did before I knew for certain I would be working on the Big Joy Project. But it was so obvious that the Universe had answered my question and provided me with just the opportunity I needed that I went for it. Two days later I gave my notice with confidence that either the Big Joy Project or another source of income would come through. And it did. In fact the Big Joy Project turned out to be more inspiring and more rewarding than I had first imagined. On top of that, instead of working four days a week, I was now working with Stephen only one day a week for roughly the same pay. This gave me enormous amounts of time to work on my own writing projects, while still supporting myself financially.

That was a real life example of how asking the right question changed my life. Singer/songwriter Ani Difranco has a verse in one of her songs that says, "If you don't ask the right question, every answer seems wrong. I was a terrible waitress so I started writing songs." While I don't believe that there is a wrong question, it is my experience that certain questions lead you to other questions. Asking one and then another often takes you to the heart of what is the real mystery for you at this time. Getting to the heart of what you really want to know is something we will explore in depth in chapter 3, but for now let me say that your "real" question is the one you don't know the answer to. Often these questions are practical, like mine in the flower shop: I had wanted to know how I could do what I needed to do without regret. These are frequently the nuts-and-bolts, practical questions that can actually change your life—the answers cause you to evolve, to expand your life to include new experiences. At the very least the answers provide you with insight into yourself that leads you in the direction you really want to go.

In my case for example, once I started asking myself why I hadn't left the flower shop, I could tell that I was afraid to leave. Once I was aware of that fear, I was able to get at what was the heart of the matter for me: *How can I do what I know I need to do without regret?* Understanding my fear helped me to prepare for the response and to frame my question in such a way that the response provided what I needed.

As I mentioned, when I hit on the right question, I felt a tangible relief in my body. It was like, *Aha! That's the real mystery! This is the answer that I do not know.*

Let me tell you, when I got that email about the part-time work, I thought, *Well, all right! That was fast!* Ask the right question, the personal mystery that you want solved right now and, presto, the solution appears.

✳

Identify whom you're asking

Other than making a specific statement, another way that you can align with the highest good is to identify whom you are talking to. You're not calling out to just anyone who has an idea (see previous bank robbing solution). You want to talk to those who have in mind the best solution for you.

Although I sometimes address my question to my guides (my personal spirit helpers), or God, or the Universe, I find most often I speak to what I call my Highest Self.

I'm very well acquainted with the part of me that I identify as my Highest Self—my best me. I've spent years getting to know her and learning to discern not only how she feels but also how I can access her when I need her. I've learned that the combination of regular meditation and physical exercise keeps me in tune with her; it grounds me in my body so that I can bring the knowledge of my Highest Self into my life. Over the years I've learned to recognize her characteristics. To me she always appears as a benevolent portion of myself. When I am operating from her core, no matter what is happening I feel very calm, at ease, and joyous. She has other qualities that I rely upon as well. For example she not only knows everything about me and where I am going, but she is also in touch with the highest notion for every outcome. She sees the big picture, and emits only those feelings that are best for everyone. For instance, she is never petty or jealous. Above all she always knows my best course of action for accomplishing what I actually came to this earth to do and whom to turn to when I need help.

I identify this part of myself as my soul. Among her other qualities is an ability to see and understand the future. She is the deepest part of my being, the one who has been around for so long that she knows all—or at least she knows a million times more than small Aimée does. She sees my life and its small happenings with a bird's eye view. She appreciates it for what it is bringing me, but she never gets bogged down in anything specific or heavy that my small self is feeling. She simply smiles and watches.

Because I feel so connected with her, my soul is the part of myself I often turn to for answers. When I need mysteries solved or solutions presented I often put things in her hands. I know her. I trust her. She always guides me to that which is in my own best interest.

The person or being you identify with may be someone or something else entirely. My mother always uses the word *God*. For her, the highest knowledge and highest experiences come from the feeling that she has for God and, even more specifically, for Jesus. This is her main connection to the expanded knowledge, and it's all that she needs. Each one of us has tangible and personal connection with the Divine that looks a little different from everyone else's. For you, it may be God, or the Creator; for another it may be Allah, or the Universe, or Great Spirit. It is not the name or the descriptive words you use that matter; it is the feeling of connection, the feeling of peace and ease you have in reference to this force. When you do your questioning, you are looking for the source that provides you with a feeling of benevolence and ease. If you refer to it with the words *Highest Self* one day and *God* or *Goddess* the next day, it does not matter. What is most important is that you are aligning yourself with what brings you the greatest sense of serenity.

Above all, we know that the source you want to address has foresight and healthy, positive answers to the questions you are asking. It sees truth, solutions, and perfection, where you sometimes get only glimpses. If it helps you to give it the name Spirit, Bob, Gretta, or Jesus, then do so. If you want it to remain nameless, that's fine too.

The most important thing here is to start your process by taking a moment to align yourself with your greatest good. Before you begin, you could choose to make a statement of intention or to address the Divine in terms of your own personal connection to it. You may also choose, as I do, to begin invoking the Divine a little differently every time. The manner in which you do it is less important than that you do it. Tuning your radar to this station is the very important first step in your process of getting answers. It's the safety net you'll rely on later when you get your answers (especially if they're different than what you thought you wanted). Not only does it assure you that your answers come from the best place, but tuning into the highest also gives you the security that everything is being taken into account. The vision of Spirit/God/ the Universe is always beyond your own. When you align with the highest good, you leave room for the possibilities that you might not know what's best and you might not have all of the details yet. We can't always see every-thing that is coming down the pike.

When I took the work for the Big Joy Project, for instance, I was just think-ing of a way to keep the income rolling in. What the Universe knew was that I also needed more time to write this book, and that Big Joy would be inspiring to me in other ways. We often started our work sessions by reading poetry, and this re-intro-duction of poetry into my life on a regular basis prompted me to seek out more po-etry and also get back to writing it myself. One of the main messages of the project was "Follow Your Own Weird," which was totally uplifting to me. It was a constant reminder to do whatever it is that makes me tick—to seek out the unique things that I love—it reminded me that, no matter what they are, these are the things that have the most value for me and add beauty to my life and that following these things is important! When you align with the highest, you leave room for juicy, delicious details that you probably wouldn't have thought of yourself, like working for an or-ganization that promotes poetry and uniqueness! And you know you can count on your answers because they aren't just any answers, they are the answers that are best for you—meaning that answers that provide you with the greatest joy. Aligning with the highest good is the step that makes that happen.

Before we move on to the second step, "Ask the Question," let's review.

Review

* There are many possible solutions to any given problem. You want the one that is best for you.

* Aligning with the Highest is the step that ensures you get these answers — the ones that bring about your greatest joy and happiness.

* You can do this by making an intention statement (remember, "So your intention, so your attainment") before you ask your question. That statement would go something like I only receive answers that are in line with my highest good. Or, *I only receive answers that serve the highest good of all.*

* You can also align with the highest good by choosing to address your question to your personal name for and connection with the Divine.

* Aligning with the highest good is like your safety net. It becomes especially important when you get answers that aren't what you'd thought they'd be. Because you've made that alignment, you can trust the answers you receive. Spirit knows more than you, and recognizing that enables you to accept even the things that you do not know yet.

* All of this happens before you move on to the next step, asking the question!

CHAPTER 2

Ask the Question

The most startling realization that I had with the *Getting Answers*, process came at a point when I didn't know what I was looking for. For some time I'd had the distinct impression that some event or person or thing was missing from my life, but I couldn't quite identify what it was. It wasn't that I was unhappy. On the contrary, my life seemed to be moving along quite swimmingly. But internally I felt that something indefinable was missing.

"I feel like something is calling me," I said to a friend one day, "but I don't know what it is." The sensation was so strong it was almost tangible. It began as a small tingle of awareness and, over many months, grew to the feeling that I was playing a game of hide-and-seek with something distinct yet unidentifiable. I could practically see "the thing," whatever it was, but it still felt just out of the reach of my consciousness.

I told a friend, "It's like there is something up ahead, hiding in the bushes. It pops out at me and dances invitingly, but by the time I get there, it's gone."

Fortunately this friend was also a healer. She was doing some bodywork on me at the time, and she said to me point blank, "You can know what it is."

"I can?" At first I was sort of shocked by this revelation. Then the certainty of her words sunk into me. "Yes, I can know what it is. In fact it wants me to know—that's why it's there."

It was a notion that I had never considered. Just the surety of it felt like a revelation. I could know what was calling me. I could name it, face it, look it straight in the eye—and then—if I knew what it was, I could find it or have it. I wouldn't have to spend my whole life trying to identify what it was. The mysterious game could end. I *could* know what it was.

The moment I left this bodywork session was when I discovered the crazily simple and yet revolutionary next step in this process: Ask the question.

Hello! In hindsight it seems obvious. And yet it was so straightforward that it had never occurred to me. Ask what it is—it's that simple.

"What is calling me?" I said aloud as I was walking to my car. "What is calling me?"

For days I walked around with that question burning inside me. I wrote it in my journal. I said it in my head and aloud to myself whenever I thought of it. I asked it again and again.

I suppose, in hindsight, it was the blessing of having this knowledge escape me for so long that made me feel patient with the process. The sensation of something calling me had been building for such a length of time that it didn't occur to me to expect a response immediately. I didn't know if it would take a day or a week. Just asking the question was such a different experience that I felt content. Deep inside I knew my friend had been right: I could know.

It was three days before the answer finally showed up. *My people*, I thought, *I am missing my people.* I knew immediately that I wasn't talking about just any people. I had lots of wonderful friends. But I felt there were some people—my soul posse, if you will--who weren't yet present in my life. I knew what these connections felt like because I had already met some of them. And to me it felt clear that there was a part of my posse—my soul family—that was calling me.

Knowing this answer provided me with tremendous relief. In this case, there wasn't anything I could do specifically to speed up the process. Or at least I didn't ask that. Just understanding what the missing element was sent a huge wave of ease through my body, and that felt like enough. Simply put, I was looking for my soul family, and I felt quite sure they were also looking for me. It was the beginning of 2009 when I had this realization, so as part of my goals and intentions for the year, I included, "find my family."

Getting the answer to this question was a new type of experience for me. Up to this point most of my questions had been about how to get what I wanted. I was used to ascertaining what I wanted and then asking about how to get it. This incident of discovering an answer that had eluded me for so many months opened up a whole new level of getting answers that I hadn't even known was an option. I realized that if I could get the answer to something that had been that mysterious to me for so long, I could get the answer to anything.

Several months later I was having coffee with a new friend. A friend who, I might add, is very definitely a part of my soul posse. She and I were talking about Getting Answers when she said, "Don't you need to include a chapter on believing in the process?"

"No," I said immediately. "Believing is not necessary."

"Really?" she said with obvious relief

"Really." I said

And I'm sure that it doesn't. One morning a few years ago I was sitting in my office looking at my bank statements online. At that point in my life I understood very little about how to manage my money properly. Looking at my bank account was always a little baffling. I didn't know an easy way to coordinate the timing of the incoming money with the outgoing bill paying. I was sure there must be a straight-forward way, but for the life of me I didn't know what it was. As I was sitting there at my desk, I pondered, *How can I manage my money better?*

A few hours later someone actually said these words to me: "Can I give you a few tips on how to manage your money better?" Sure I was standing in the bank, and the person who offered the advice worked there. But I hadn't voiced my question to her. I was just sitting at her desk while she checked into a few other things for me when, off the top of her head, she offered to help me learn how to manage my money better—using exactly the same phrase that I had used that morning. In all of my life, this was the one and only time anyone had ever said that to me.

I was so eager for the answer, I practically shouted, "YES!" In just minutes she walked me through a process that I could do online to insure that not only did the money go out when it was actually in the account, but also that my balance would reflect any withdrawals immediately. I would never again have to wonder if the balance on the screen matched what I had left in my account.

That morning when I thought the question, I didn't have faith that the answer would arrive. I wasn't even thinking in those terms. I had a question—and that was it.

I made another discovery several months ago as I was looking through my journals that for me cemented the understanding about how asking a question always produces an answer. Even though I'm a writer, and I write every day, I seldom go back and read what I've written, at least in my personal notebooks. So I was doing that rare act of sitting down and reading through some sections of my private thoughts, when I realized something fascinating. Every question I had ever asked, and believe me my journal was rife with them, had been answered. *What can I do to make more money right now? What is the best way to resolve my housing situation? How can I get re-inspired? What is this situation trying to show me?* As I looked through my journals at the myriad of questions, I saw that every single one of them had been answered. Some of them, in fact the majority of them, had been resolved without even my conscious awareness. I wrote the question down and then I forgot about it. Some were made obsolete, or resolved, by the arrival of another solution. But whether or not I had been aware, I had lived my way into the answer to every single question I had ever asked. It was like a demonstration of one of my favorite quotes by Rainer Maria Rilke:

> I beg of you to have patience with everything unresolved in your heart and try to love the questions themselves as if they were locked rooms or books written in a very foreign language. Don't search for the answers, which could not be given to you now, because you would not be able to live them. And the point is, to live everything. Live the questions now. Perhaps then, someday far in the future, you will gradually, without ever noticing it, live your way into the answer.

What startled me was that I *had* been given the answer to every single question I had asked. Even if I had personally forgotten about the question by the time I received the answer, the Universe had not forgotten. God had remembered that I asked—and the answer, without exception, had been provided. It never failed.

It was then that the thought began to dawn on me, *What if I started to consciously ask questions and actually wait for their response?* If I get the answer to every question I ask, how much more powerful would the process be if I started to identify the key questions for myself and actually expect a response?

That is how the second step in this process was born. Ask the question. Now remember—if I may point out the obvious here—this step is not "ask question/receive answers." It is "ask the question" period.

Framing your issues or concerns into a question form is essential. Why is the asking so important? Well, as you undoubtedly know, there are many puzzling things in life. For instance, I have no idea how the engine in my car is built. I also know very little about gardening. But unless I take the time to ask, I am not likely to receive information about these topics. When you ask a question, you indicate to the Universe, loudly and clearly, *This is information I want!* For instance, chatting with your friend about how your job doesn't have health benefits is very different than saying, *Highest Self, How can I find a job with health benefits?* When you ask a question, you send a signal, a bright wide beam to the Universe. It's like a spotlight that says, *Answer needed here please!* It lets your guides (or your "peeps" as I like to call them), God, or your Highest Self know that this is not just idle speculation or a commonplace remark on the happenings of the world—it is something that needs addressing. It puts both your conscious and your unconscious to the task of finding a response immediately. You are looking for an answer. You want a response. You want to know—how to find a job you like with health benefits, for example, or how to increase your income, or how you can easily move to Paris next winter, or whatever.

Something that I know from my own experience is that it is easier to find the answer if you know that you're looking for it! It is also easier to interpret the messages your life brings when you have asked something specific. Your guides appreciate your free will. You have the right to sit as long as you want—days, months, or even years—ruminating over something, just letting it be without asking for a solution. That is your option. You can stay as long as you want with the thought, *This sucks* or *I wish this were different* before moving to *How do I solve this? or What can be done?* However, the moment that you say, *I need help!* or *How can I fix this?* the Universe is ready and at attention. That higher power will do whatever it takes to get you the answer that best serves you, guaranteed. It wants you to know. If you want to know, it wants you to know.

So take Rilke's advice and love the questions. Remember it is this little query that is going to provide for you. If it helps you, you can look at the question like a precious gem. Eventually it is the light striking this gem that will lead you to what you really want—your answer. So enjoy the process of asking—feel the words roll around on your tongue, let them fill a page of your journal, just revel in the feeling of your question taking form in the Universe. Understand that without a doubt, it is your question that will lead you to what you really want—the knowing. Live the question, knowing for certain that when the time is right the answer will arrive.

Recommended practices

Have fun with this step. You can write out the questions in fancy or inspiring ways. You can post them in your bathroom and repeat them out loud when you are there. You can sing them in the shower. Scribe them on post it notes and stick them to your steering wheel. Repeat them as a mantra when you are waiting at a stoplight. Hang them under magnets on your refrigerator so that you'll notice them whenever you open the door. Do whatever you are inspired or moved to do to help yourself love and repeat these questions. I highly recommend setting aside a page in your journal (maybe near the end) just for your questions. (If you don't have a journal, get a little notebook specifically for questions.) Write each question you ask, along with the date. It's very helpful to keep this record. Not only does this allow you to track what you've asked, it will also help you see later how it has been answered. You can notice for instance that on this date you asked this question, and two days later such-and-such happened. It's fun to look back later, even months later, and see how your life was reshaped because of the questions you asked. Sometimes after a while you forget what you've asked—but the Universe never does. So having all of this noted is fun for tracking the results.

If you're not exactly clear on what you want to ask or how to ask it, don't worry. I'm going to give you some tips on that next. But before we do that, let's review the second step.

Review

* Asking the question is a step in itself. Because it is so obvious, it can be easily overlooked. However, it is the most necessary step in leading you effortlessly to an answer.

* You will get an answer to every question you ask, guaranteed, whether you believe it or not, or even whether you are paying attention—the answers will arrive.

* It is the act of asking that sends the beacon to the Universe letting it know that you would like a response.

* Live the question and love the questions. They point you to what you most want: your answer.

* Have fun with this! You can post your questions around the house or in places you frequent to remind yourself to ask them.

* Keep a record. Set aside a page in your journal or keep a specific notebook just for questions. Be sure to always note the date you asked. This will help you notice later how the Universe responded to your request.

CHAPTER 3

Getting to the Heart of What You Really Want to Know

When I teach the Getting Answers process, it's at this point that a lot of my students say they're not really sure what to ask. Usually people have a general idea of what's going wrong in their life, but they're not sure how to frame it as a question. It may seem surprising, but because we're not used to phrasing issues as questions, this often stumps people. This chapter will help you address this difficulty. You can ask anything, absolutely anything. But you'll probably find that some answers are more satisfying than others. This is because these are the answers that you most want to know.

Recently, a client of mine told me how for some time she had been pondering whether this particular man was her life partner. They had been together for years. They had separated some time back in order to take work on different sides of the country, but they'd remained very close. Because of their strong connection, my client wondered if he was the man for her. Right after she applied the process of getting answers, asking if this man was her life partner, she had a conversation with a girlfriend. In this conversation she discovered that truly, at this moment in time, even if this man was her life partner, she didn't feel ready to move forward with him into that kind of commitment. She saw that the two of them were in such different places right now—not just physically but also mentally—that even if ultimately they were a good match, at this time the information was beside the point.

I believe that asking the question is what pointed her to what she really wanted to know. In this case, it also pointed her to how irrelevant that particular question was for her. Sometimes what we think we want to know isn't at all what we want to know. But asking, even asking an irrelevant question, gets the process going and helps us define that. In my client's case, asking the question, and the shaping of her life that ensued, caused her to drop the question altogether. For her, this was no small thing, because this was a subject that had been haunting her for months, one that she was finally able to put to rest.

In many cases, by the time my clients come to me, and certainly if they have spoken with me beforehand, they have very specific questions. I encourage people to be as specific as possible with their questions, because this is how you get specific answers. In my own life I've noticed that occasionally the process of understanding what I'm truly looking for takes time and feels a bit nebulous. This chapter is intended to help you move through that and get specific more quickly. I've observed that oftentimes when I feel stuck in life, it's because I don't know exactly what I'm looking for, what I want. This chapter includes techniques that I use to help myself get unstuck and also get clear on what I really want to know, so that the solutions that appear in my life truly reflect what I am looking for.

Identifying your needs

The best way to get the answers you want is to understand what you really want to know. When I experience dissatisfaction, I sometimes feel it's because I'm not asking the right question for me at this time. Now when I say *the right question,* I mean two things. First, this is often a question you don't know the answer to and, secondly, it is usually indicative of an experience you want to have but are not (yet) having.

When I knew I needed to leave the flower shop, for instance, I understood that I needed to do that, but I didn't know how to do it in a way that would be easeful for me. So I asked, *How can I leave the flower shop gracefully, easefully, and without regret?* And when I asked about managing my money better, this was an experience that I felt I was ready to have but was not yet having.

The best way to get to the bottom of what you want to know is to do some self-inquiry. You ask yourself questions until you come to the one you don't know the answer to. Or you could ask yourself questions until you have a good understanding of what you want to create, and then ask how to do it.

Below, I have listed some of the questions that I ask myself. Some of these queries are similar, but they all use slightly different language to come at the same issue. I find that sometimes one angle works better than others, so I've included several options to get you started. You can use these questions to help you start identifying your current needs and desires.

— *What do I want more than anything else right now?*
— *What do I want to change in my life?*
— *What do I believe would make my life better?*
— *What is happening in my life right now?*
— *What is happening in my life that is working well?*
— *What is happening in my life that is not working well?*
— *What is baffling me?*
— *What do I want or need right now?*

— *What is it about that particular thing that is (or sounds) satisfying?*
— *Why do I want that?*
— *What is important to me about that thing that I want?*

I've noticed that if I'm stuck in negative thinking or I'm having a hard time envisioning positive outcomes, it is easier to start with negative questions because that is where my mind is. You can start with the question, *What is happening in my life that is not working well?* But don't stop there. The goal here is to come up with what you actually want—so if you use the negative side of the question, you must flip it around again to find its opposite. Get it? Once you identify what isn't working, then you ask yourself what the opposite or antidote of that is to find out what you really want.

Going deeper with questions like *Why do I want that?* or *What is important to me about that?* often sheds even more light on the subject. For example, you might answer, *My life would be better if I didn't have to spend so much time cleaning my house.* By asking yourself the follow-up question—*Why is that important to me?*—you might find out that you want to spend more time working in your garden or playing with your children. Your real question then might be this: *How do I find more time to do work in my garden or play with my children?* It might involve having help cleaning your house—or it might not. Solutions are truly infinite. The Universe can find all sorts of innovative ways to get you what you need. The benefit of knowing what that is, is that you can get it sooner. If for example you found a way to get more help cleaning your house, but what you really wanted was to spend more time creating and planting your garden, the house cleaning solution may not suit. But likely, if you got what you were really craving—more time to grow your flowers—you wouldn't mind so much about the dusting. I don't know, maybe you want both. You can have both, but it's easier to get it if you know what you want.

Again the goal of doing this self-inquiry is to help you identify what I'll call here the "real question," just to differentiate it from the self-inquiry you are doing. This is the question that you need the Universe's help on—it's the one that currently stumps you and whose response will truly change your life for the better. Getting as clear as possible on where you are currently and what you feel is working and not working helps you identify the changes you want to make. Because you get the answer to every question you ask, the clearer you are on what you want to know, or what you are ready to experience in your life, the more efficient your real question will be. Don't worry if you don't have it right the first time—you can always ask for what you need when you realize you need it (and certainly your needs and wants will evolve over time as your life changes). But the closer you get to identifying the experience you are ready to have, the sooner your solution will arrive.

It's helpful to break it down into these pieces because sometimes we make conclusions that aren't necessarily true. For example, recently in a *Getting Answers* class, one of the students said, "I want to know how I can get a university job so that I can pay the rent on my dance studio." Actually these could be very separate issues. We know that she wants to keep her dance studio and thereby needs a way to support it. But we don't know for sure that getting a university job is going to be the best way to do that. For sure it's one option, but it might just be the only option her brain can come up with and not the only option or even the best option there is. So, breaking it down into what you really need and why this is important to you can help you shed light on what you are really looking for. Also in this woman's case, finding out what is appealing to her about a university job would help her further identify the qualities that she wants to incorporate into her money-making endeavors. This might help her recognize new options or be present to the opportunities that Spirit provides when they are offered, even if they don't look like a university job.

Another reason it's helpful to get clear on your real question is that different questions can produce vastly different answers or results. I was talking about this process recently at a National Speakers Association meeting. One of my fellow meeting attendees told me how he was very interested in getting answers, because a large portion of what he does is to help businesses come up with the right questions. He said that when he was working with Starbucks "the question of how to sell a lot of coffee beans is very different from how to create a place where people want to come and hang out." Depending on what you truly want, the result and the actions are very different.

When I feel stuck, often what I do is to start writing down and responding to questions like the ones listed above. I assess where I am currently at, what I actually feel about it, and what I would like to change or create. There are endless questions you can ask yourself in this vein—one usually leads to another. Just go with it.

Eventually, the process will lead you to a question for which you don't have an answer. Once you've identified your needs, it's usually a question like these: *How can I get this particular thing? Who can help me? What do I need to do now?* When I get to a question whose answer will change my life in the direction that I wish to go in, I find there's often a sparkle around that question. Just asking that question brings a profound silence, a silence that I sense is full of possibilities. I feel relief because I know that without a doubt this is the question I really want the answer to, and I know that the answer will come. It's only a matter of time.

Using query to learn about yourself or the experiences you want to have

In addition to using the *Getting Answers* process to produce concrete experiences (like a new job, or a new place to live,) you can also use it to find out more about yourself and to discover experiences you would like to have. It's different than the self-inquiry because again it is a question that you don't know the answer to, and your asking it actually produces a result. I think the easiest way to describe it is to give you an example.

As I mentioned in chapter 2, there was a time when I felt something was missing from my life, but I didn't know what this was. To me it felt like an experience of my life was calling me. So I started asking, *What is calling me?* This question was akin to *What is missing from my life right now?* Since I didn't know what I really wanted, it was in asking this question that I became clear on what that was. The answer that I received was my people, or my "soul posse," as I like to call them. I felt that this was definitely related to my friendships, but a big part of it was related to a life partner and family for me. I understood that there was this important part of my people missing in my life and it felt like several of them were future family members of mine. It was actually this process that pointed out to me that for perhaps the first time in my life I felt truly ready for a life-long partnership and family.

At the time I didn't feel in any rush. For me, just identifying that was a huge relief. Over the months that followed, I watched how some pivotal and soulful friends appeared in my life. And I also started to take a more serious look at what a life-long romantic partnership meant to me. I began to do some self-inquiry about what I want in a partner and what I thought such a union would bring me. I was interested in finding out the answer to these questions for several reasons. First, I believe it's easier to get what you want, or recognize it when it comes, when you actually know what that is. Second, I was interested to find out what I thought having a partner would bring to me because I had never really examined this before. Third, I believe the easiest way to attract what you want is to be that yourself. I felt that if I knew what I was actually looking for, I could not only start to recognize its current existence in my life, I could also make sure I was owning and creating those qualities in myself.

In this case I used the *Getting Answers* process to go deeper into myself and to find out more about what was really important to me, about what I felt I really wanted and needed, and then to actually create the experience of it within myself.

Asking myself a series of specific questions related to this issue led me to some pivotal information about myself and what I was looking for. It also guided me to other real questions like these: *Is there such a thing as true love and partnership? What does that feel like?*

Now, as I've said, every question receives an answer, and these intangible questions are no different. When I began asking these questions, I started to actually feel the sensations of what a true partnership would be like for me. I was not only identifying its qualities, I was experiencing them in my body.

The best way that I have of explaining this is that I started to feel as though this partnership were actually happening—right now! I was able to describe in detail, to myself and even to my friends, what such a partnership felt like and how it felt for me to be in one. I could do this because I was experiencing the very same sensations I would experience were I actually in this partnership. I also saw visions in my mind that gave me very specific feelings and details about this relationship's qualities.

Because many of these sensations and understandings were new to me, I knew that I was having them as a direct result of the questions I had been asking.

Truthfully, I had never been in this kind of partnership before, and I hadn't thought a lot about what that would look or feel like. But I could feel it then, as clearly as if my man were in the next room waiting for me.

This is an example of how I used the *Getting Answers* process to understand things not only about myself but about the experiences I wanted to manifest. They weren't the kind of questions that produced something concrete and immediate like a job offer, but they were key to my understanding of myself and my desires. At the very least this experience gave me a taste of what I'm looking for. Knowing what it feels like goes a long way toward actually getting it. And I also believe this experience will play an important role in my own recognition of this partnership when I arrive at it.

So you can use the *Getting Answers* process to produce tangible results in your life, and you can also use it to gain a greater understanding of yourself and of the experiences you are hoping to have. This knowledge, in turn, can lead you to all sorts of questions about how to manifest those things.

The bottom line is this: the easiest way to get what you really want is to know what it is. To help define this for yourself, start with self-inquiry. Once again, ask yourself questions until you find one you don't know the answer to or until you discover what you really want. Then you can ask how to get it.

Next, we explore the first secret ingredient in the *Getting Answers* process, but before we do, let's review.

Review

* Some answers are more satisfying than others, because these are the answers that you really want to know.

* Asking specific questions gets you specific answers. Therefore, the more specific you can be about what you want, the more your response will re-

flect that Another way to say that is the clearer you are about what you want, the more likely you are to get it.

✳ Sometimes feeling stuck is related to not knowing what you really want. It's possible that you haven't been asking the right question (or the one that you truly want to know). To find the right question, start doing some self-inquiry.

✳ Self-inquiry can help you get unstuck or clarify what you really want. Ask yourself questions like these: *What do I want more than anything else right now? What do I feel would make my life better?*

✳ Ask until you come to a point where you don't know the answer (that is your "real question") or until you have identified clearly what you really want. Then you can ask how to get it.

✳ Asking questions or getting to the bottom of what you really want also helps you recognize the answers when they arrive—even if they look differently than you thought.

✳ Asking questions does shape your life. Different questions produce different results. That's one more reason to know what you want. Then you can shape your question into the one that you really want to know.

✳ You can also use questions to find out more about yourself, or to produce experiences that you would like to manifest.

CHAPTER 4

Secret Ingredient #1: Patience

"Have patience with everything unresolved in your heart," Rilke counsels. Now that's some good, solid, ageless advice. Remember when I said it's guaranteed the answer will show up guaranteed? Well it's true. What's unknown is the when. Now I don't want to get you discouraged here right off the bat. It's been my experience that answers don't take long in coming. Nonetheless, the truth is that neither you nor I have any control over the timing of the Universe. In fact, we have barely an inkling (and that is being very generous) as to how it actually works. This being the case, I've included this chapter to introduce you to one of your primary allies, a secret ingredient that will help this process go more smoothly for you: Patience.

Applying patience can sometimes be very challenging, and, believe me, I know all about this. For the vast majority of my life patience was something I actually loathed. When I was growing up my mother used to say, "Aimée, patience is a virtue." I didn't care. To me patience seemed like a hideous monster hiding inside the clothes of something that looked desirable. I wasn't fooled. I associated this so-called virtue with one of two things. For me it signaled either a form of settling for less (which I was determined not to do) or (worse yet) a glaring lack of imagination.

I can now see that neither of these views left any room for the work of Spirit. It took me a long time to learn that rather than being a loathsome creature, patience is an absolutely necessary companion in life.

I'm sure you understand. I'll bet if you were to take a serious look at your life… Anyway, when I look at mine, I see that things don't always move at the speed I prefer. Believe me, as a psychic the art of waiting is a lesson that I go over and over again and again. And again. Imagine how frustrating it can be when you know certain things are going to happen, but you still have to wait for them to occur! This is just like you and your answer! Even when you know it's coming, you still have to practice the fine art of waiting for it. That is why it is important to understand patience.

It took me a long time to get that patience was an ally to me. As I mentioned, I went years of my life thinking of it as a monster in disguise. What I've discovered now is that not only is patience not a beast, it is actually a valuable and trustworthy friend that helps (not hinders) me in getting what I want. In this case we are talking about getting answers. Patience is the first secret ingredient that helps us get the answers we want, that is, the practical knowledge that will help us move our lives forward or help us understand certain things about our lives. So, here is what I suggest.

Understand that patience is not something you are forced to apply as you wait for what you want. Patience is actually your loving companion. It is a very wise and reflective friend who is—gloriously!—on your side. To illustrate I'll contrast patience with imagination, which is how I originally pitted it in my youthful mind.

Pretend they are both sentient beings. (This will also help you see Patience as a friend.) Patience and Imagination are very different. For example, unlike Imagination, Patience doesn't shout out any answer that comes to her, in fact she rarely says anything at all. She takes her time. She doesn't want you to have just any solution; she wants you to have the one that is perfect for you. The irony lies in the fact that without Patience, Imagination could hardly do anything at all. The truth is they are not avowed enemies; they are indispensable cohorts.

Envision the dialogue between Imagination and Patience. Say you need a birthday cake.

"I know, let's stop at the gas station and get one of those Hostess cupcakes," Imagination shouts out. "Or what about those little puffy biscuits we've got in the freezer—we could use one of those and put some whipped cream and a candle on it!

Ummm… How about drawing a cake on a piece of paper," Imagination chirps eagerly, "and then setting it on fire for the candles!"

Imagination's job is to come up with as many solutions as it possibly can. Nothing is off limits, anything and everything goes—this is her strength. Patience's role, however, is to sort through the options, taking the time to bring together the perfect one.

"*Hmmm,*" Patience replies, "let's start with some eggs." She begins to smile. She's thinking. She's slowly compiling the elements and waiting for just the right answer.

Patience makes the cake.

Imagination may come up with the ideas, but it's Patience who does the work. And let me tell you, the cake that Patience creates is out of this world! It makes your mouth water and your taste buds explode in wonder. It's the kind of result that brings about a shut-your-eyes, sit-back-in-your-chair, *mmmmmm,* heaven-on-earth experience. The kind of experience you remember for the rest of your life.

Imagination can come up with wild and amazing ideas all on her own, but it's Patience who puts them all together. Planning and plotting out just the perfect combination, Patience works in silence until the final masterpiece is revealed. Patience never gives anything away until the timing is just right.

Together, Patience and Imagination are a fantastic team. But without Patience, Imagination can do little more than… well, imagine.

So bringing this back to our *Getting Answers* process, it's patience that we can use as our secret ingredient after we ask our question. Understand that patience is not only at your side ready to assist you. It is behind the scenes helping Great Spirit or the Universe put together the most delicious mouth-watering package for you. Simply put, patience helps create the best results. And as we noted at the beginning, that is what we are looking for: not just any old answer but the best results!

This outcome sometimes takes time. What I didn't know in my youth was that just because it's quiet, or you don't actually see anything happening, doesn't mean nothing is happening. A lack of any obvious result does not mean that the solution is not on the way. It just means it's not yet time for you to know about it. Just like with the cake, the Universe has got to assemble all of the ingredients and then combine them in the right way. As anyone knows eggs, flour, sugar, butter, and chocolate don't make a cake. It's how you put these raw ingredients together and how you bake them that makes the alchemy happen—that brings forth a delicacy.

With Great Spirit it seems that most of the baking happens behind the scenes. Therefore it is sometimes easy to misinterpret the silence. But just remember, ask the question and the answer will be revealed. The silence just means God—or the Universe, the Great Spirit, your Guides, or your own Highest Self—is at work. He (or She or it) is gathering and uniting the necessary combination for the perfect result. All you have to do is sit back and wait.

A little trick: Employing the art of pretend

That said, if the waiting still gets to you, here is a little trick you can play on your mind to help ease the discomfort of waiting: Pretend it has already worked out. Yep, you read that right—pretend.

Remember when I mentioned that I decided to quit the flower shop before I had heard for sure whether I would be offered work on the Big Joy Project. Well, even though I knew it was the right thing to do, I still had some butterflies in my stomach when it came to the actual waiting. So I decided to play a trick on myself to relieve my own anxiety. I told myself, quite reasonably, that no matter what, the situation would be resolved. Every situation is always resolved.

It's like this refrigerator magnet that I bought for my mom a few years ago. It says, "Everything always works out in the end. If it hasn't worked out, it's not the end." I love that. And I find it's true.

In the scheme of my life I can think of very few things (none actually come to mind) that haven't resolved themselves. In my situation with the flower shop I could see that the most probable outcome would be that I would be offered the new job. It was obvious that it truly had been an answer to my questioning. Furthermore, even if I wasn't offered this job, I knew that I wouldn't actually spend the rest of my life looking for another source of a stable income. It would all work out. It always had.

So I decided to make it easy on myself and simply pretend that it had worked out already. I figured also, that in hindsight, when it actually did all work out, I would be much happier with myself if I hadn't spent the intermittent time worrying over something that turned out well. So that is what I decided to do. Every time I felt anxious about waiting, I reminded myself that in a very short time period I would know the answer. I pretended that I was at that moment of the future when I would already know for certain how it had turned out. I let the ease of knowing settle into my bones. It felt so much better than fretting.

I recommended this technique recently to my sister. She had just been laid off from her work at National Public Radio and was uncertain about what to do next. "Look at it this way," I said to her on the phone, "It is going to work out. You are not going to spend the rest of your life without a job. If you spend your time worrying about it now, when it's all over with you will kick yourself for wasting all of that time when you could've been enjoying yourself. So just pretend it already has worked out for the best, and save your energy for more positive things right now."

She agreed, and guess what? It did work out for the best! After she left NPR, she took the time to get clear about what she wanted to do with herself—and in the end she completely switched directions. She followed a dream she'd had since childhood of owning a bed and breakfast. Instead of getting another office job, she was offered and accepted a position at a beautiful seaside B&B. It was perfect for her. The timing was serendipitous, and she was on her way to discovering more about her own personal dream.

So, even if you have to trick yourself by pretending that it has already happened, I heartily recommend that you do. It will make you so much happier, both in the short and long run. Because it will work out. It always does.

✴

Another little trick: Sitting in the waiting room with your friend Patience

Worry or impatience is a result of a fear that it won't work out. Personally, I've noticed the cues in my own life that tell me I'm starting to panic. One of the biggest clues for me happens the moment I start feeling in my body this frenetic feeling: *Oh my gosh, I've got to do something now!* When that happens, I do just the opposite. I remember that the best answers do not come on a carpet of panic or anxiety—they always come naturally and gracefully. When I'm starting to feel panicked, I remind myself that it is not time to "do something—anything!" It's time to sit back and hold the hand of my dear friend Patience.

I see myself in a waiting room. Patience is by my side. She is lovingly holding my hand making things easier for me as I wait for my answer. For Patience, there is no doubt that my number will be called, that I will get what I want. She knows, it's just a matter of time. Her skill, her forte, her out-of-this-world brilliance lies in making the wait easy, graceful, and comfortable. Because she knows soon it will be time to receive my answer, and that is precisely what we intend to do next.

But of course, first—review.

Review

* No matter what, we do not control the timing of the Universe, which is why patience is helpful.

* See Patience as a comforting friend who will make getting answers easy for you.

* Without Patience, the best solutions are rarely found.

* The best answers always come naturally and gracefully. Patience is there to help you sit through the wait.

* Trick one: If you have a hard time, pretend. Pretend you have already received your answer, because things do always work out in the end. Remember you will not spend the rest of your life waiting—this is only temporary.

* Trick two: View yourself sitting in a waiting room with your glorious friend Patience lovingly holding your hand and waiting with you easily until your answer is called.

Chapter 5

Receiving Answers

Now comes the fun part—receiving answers. As I've said before, the answers show up in your life easily and naturally, and they come as you are doing whatever it is that you do. That means—and I can't stress this enough—you don't have to work for them or strain yourself in any way to find the answers . Your job is just to sit with your friend Patience until the answers appear.

I also need to warn you that your answers are probably going to come in completely ordinary ways. From something someone says to you while you're standing in line at the post office for example, or through a song that you hear on the radio, or in a conversation you have with your Aunt Mildred's neighbor at her 90th birthday party. Answers will appear while you are living your life, whatever that looks like for you. This is part of the process that makes it such fun, and also so amazingly simple that you'll wonder why you never caught onto this before. The extraordinary often wears the clothes of the ordinary—and receiving answers is no exception.

The obvious answers

Sometimes the answer will be so obvious it will be impossible for you to miss. Like the time I mentioned earlier when I walked into my bank and the bank manager answered my question directly, using the same words I had in asking the question.

I'll give you a few more examples of this kind of unmistakable answer.

One day I asked myself, *What other avenues should I explore in my writing?* I wrote the question in my journal, and I went to the grocery store. I was standing in the bulk food aisle when a friend of mine approached me and said, "You know, you should write a short story for our radio show." No kidding. I don't even think I had spoken to another person between the time I wrote the question in my journal and when my friend found me in the bulk aisle. He knew nothing about my inquiry. He just saw me and voiced that thought, which—as it just so happened—was an answer to my question.

Another time I was considering how I could bring more artistry to my work. I had also been feeling called to find a way to expand on my one-on-one intuitive readings so that I could speak to more people at one time. I asked my question in the morning, and before noon, one of my neighbors asked if I would teach a workshop with her. She is fluent in a process called Interplay, which integrates mind, body, and spirit through playful movements and forms. She asked me if I would lead a week-end event on intuition—the idea being to integrate intuitive work and creative play!

These two answers were hard to miss. I couldn't miss them, and I find that other people receive answers in this way all the time. I'm sure that you will as well. The solutions will be direct and apparent replies to your questions, and they will appear in ways it is impossible for you to misunderstand. Someone may use the exact phrase that you used in your question or be speaking on the exact topic that you are wondering about. If you're thinking about going to Hawaii for the winter, someone may say to you, "Hey do you know anyone interested in renting a place in Hawaii this winter? We have this great place we're not going to use this year." It will be something like that. Something so obvious you cannot possibly overlook it.

These obvious answers are not the ones you will have a hard time interpreting, so I don't want to spend a lot of time on this. I just want to show you that they exist and to assure you that this is one of the ways that you will receive answers.

Answers with the signature of Spirit

There is also another way that Spirit will give you answers. These are a little subtler, but once you experience it a time or two, these answers will be as obvious as the first. In fact, I'm sure you have already had these instances in your life; you just may not have known that they were times when Spirit was talking to you. The easiest way to recognize these answers when they come is that your senses become very amplified. For a second, or however long it takes for you to receive your information, your normal way of perceiving things is heightened or in some way altered. The moment often takes on a feeling of timelessness. It feels like everything but the thing that you are being directed to notice fades into the background.

Again, I'll give you some examples.

Many years ago I was living in Port Townsend, Washington. Although I had dear friends there, it never truly felt like home to me. I loved the small town feel of it, but somehow I always felt as though I were driving through someone else's hometown, not my own. I got to a point where I began to realize that I needed to leave Port Townsend. I felt ready to find my own home even though I had no idea where that was. *Where is my home?* was the question foremost on my mind. I was standing in a girlfriend's living room one afternoon when I got my answer.

My friend was telling me about something she and some other friends had done over the weekend, and in the course of her story, she said the word *Vashon.* It totally stuck out to me. It felt like everything else she had said was in a normal voice, but for that one word she had picked up a mini-megaphone and spoken through it right into my ear. The word Vashon was still echoing in my head when I interrupted her.

"Wait. What's that?" I asked. "What's *Vashon?*"

"Oh it's the island where Mark and Dana live," she said, and continued her story.

It was that one word in her story that provided me with the answer I was looking for. Following that lead, I went to check out the island of Vashon. As soon as I landed on the island, doors started opening for me, and a few months later I made the move. Since the moment I arrived, this little island community has felt like home to me in a way that no other place ever has. And all it took for me to get here was asking the question and living my life. No extra hoopla needed.

The truth is, God, Spirit, and your benevolent helpers and guides are speaking to you all of the time. They want you to have the answers to your questions. They do. They want you to have whatever information will make your life easier, better, more fun, more satisfying, happier, etc. They want you to know what is in your best interest and they will use any means necessary to get through to you.

Several months ago I was speaking to a friend when I received another important message. I had been thinking about Europe a lot during that time, Ireland specifically. This was not long after I had made the realization that I was looking for my soul family. As I thought about Ireland, I considered the possibility of going there for an extended visit—like six months to a year or something. I was playing with different ideas in my mind, considering what would be best for me overall and wondering how or if these ideas fit into finding my soul family. As I was telling my girlfriend about this one morning, I got my answer. In response to what I had just told her, she looked at me thoughtfully, cocked her head to one side, and then said, "It would be a mistake for you to think that anything you need is anywhere other than here."

As she said those words, I heard them in what I sometimes call the voice-of-God tone. It wasn't that my friend had changed her voice at all. But the words reverberated in my head, echoing throughout my whole body as though she'd spoken through a microphone. I felt like I had just heard the voice of the Divine, through the lips of my girlfriend Mary Kay.

The words were still resounding in my mind a half an hour later as I got in my car. Sitting in the driver's seat, I spoke them out loud to myself for the first time. At that moment my back windshield wiper whirled to life. Now this might not have been significant except for the fact that it hadn't worked for the last six months. I laughed out loud as the wiper thumped across the dry window like a dog's wagging tail: *You got the message! Yay! We're so happy! Yes, EVERYTHING you need is RIGHT HERE.* I could practically hear my spirit guides shout!

Like I said, your benevolent helpers—God, your Highest Self, whatever you want to call your version of the Highest—will use whatever means necessary to get through to you. Nothing, not even inanimate objects, is off limits!

Not too long ago I was sitting in the work place of a friend of mine. She had just separated from her partner of 15 years. Not only did they own a home together, they also ran and operated a business together. We were sitting inside her office one evening when she confided in me that she was considering leaving the business altogether. At that moment the lights flickered. For one second the lights actually went off and back on again in her office. Spirit was talking to her. Yes! Leave the *business!* it practically shouted. *That is a good idea for you!* How did we know that was the answer? Because it happened in direct response to what she had just been talking about. The timing was precisely aligned with her words. Now if she had been saying something like, "I think there is more for me to learn here. I don't know why but I feel as though I need to stick this out a little longer," and then the lights flickered—the message would have been entirely different. We knew what the answer was because of what we had been talking about when the lights went off. In my experience messages with inanimate objects are used to confirm whatever has just been happening. Spirit will not try to make you guess what it means—it guides you by responding to what you have just been saying or doing. The specifics of the answer lay in what you have just thought, said, or done; and the participation of the inanimate object signals an affirmation to that response.

Messages are not hard to interpret. They are easy to understand when they come. And the truth is answers are always showing up in your life—even if you are unaware of them. In the next chapter I will give you some tips on broadening your awareness so that you don't miss the solutions when they arrive, but for now let me say that you need not worry about this too much. If you don't hear the response the first time, the answer will come again.

I remember one time I was trying to figure out what to do about my living situation. I lived in a beautiful house that I adored, but my roommate had decided that he was ready to leave the island we lived on. I knew that I didn't want to extend that much of my energy paying for the whole house on my own, and yet I loved the place so much that I was loathe to move. I spent several months looking for a roommate. I put up signs all over town and on the Internet.

I remember the day that I received my first message about the situation, I was a talking to a potential roommate. We were sitting at my dining room table. First she confided in me that although she loved my place and the two of us got along very well, she had just been offered a place to live by a friend of hers for hardly any rent. It was an offer that she just couldn't refuse. Then she gave me my message. Out of the blue she told me a story about a time in her life when she had to move out of a big beautiful house that she loved. She shared how, although she had been really sad to do it, it was obviously the right answer for her at that time. As I listened to her story, I felt a twinge of Spirit's signature, I'm-talking-to-you sensation. But still I wasn't sure. The truth is that I didn't want to leave that house so I wasn't entirely ready to hear that message. I was holding on so tightly to the outcome I wanted, not neces-sarily the one that would be best for me, that Spirit was having a hard time getting a message through. Since I didn't want to act hastily on a message that wasn't what I was hoping for, I decided to wait to be sure.

Not long afterward I got a message that I couldn't deny. It came in the form of a song. One morning I woke up with the song "House of the Rising Son" playing loudly in my head. I hadn't heard that song in about a decade and now, suddenly, I couldn't get it out of my head. So I knew it was a message. Since I couldn't remember all of the words I looked it up on the Internet. When I found the lyrics, the answer was obvious.

There is a house in New Orleans

They call the risin' sun

It's been the ruin of many a poor girl

And me, oh God, I'm one

A house ruining someone! Hel-lo! I was so fixated on my adoration of my house that I couldn't see it was ruining me. Choosing to pay a hefty rent on my own every month, waiting for a roommate who never showed up—it was literally ruining me financially. I needed something simpler. I needed to move.

Now that wasn't the answer I had been hoping for, but I trusted it. It felt right. By that point, I had had enough experience with getting answers to know that even if I don't understand it at the time, the answers I get always direct me toward my highest good—that is whatever is truly best for me, or whatever brings me the most joy and satisfaction. That time my guides weren't taking any chances. I can only think that they must have been trying to get through to me for a long time because they left that song playing in my head uninterrupted for four whole days! What else could I do? Move out!

Before I made that move, I couldn't have imagined the depth of peace and simplicity that leaving that house would provide me. When I moved, it was as if a ton of bricks was lifted off my shoulders. I found a great place to live right next to friends in a cute little cottage (well, a yurt) that cost a third as much as the house I had been living in. Not only were the surroundings beautiful, but I was able to save money and make progress on what had already been one of my goals—financial health and success.

The answer I received supported me not only in that moment, but also in the long run, helping me realize my larger objectives. Spirit knew my goals and also knew what was coming. That answer led me to the solution that was best for me— not only in that moment but also in the long run. Decreasing my rent enabled me to work less and write more—the book you are holding is a result of that decision.

Your answers will also point you to what is in your own highest interest. That is why you do the first step of aligning with the highest good. The more you play with this process the more you will learn to recognize easily the ways that Spirit speaks to you, or gives you your answers. Of course there will always be surprises— that's part of the fun—but there will be some similarities as well.

For me, for example, I often receive messages through songs. That's part of why I knew that song was a message. I pay attention to the ones that pop into my head unbidden or stay in my head for long periods of time. I know a woman who receives the bulk of her answers in the mail. She will go to the mailbox and the answer to something she has been pondering will be there in writing. It could be the words on the envelope of a sales letter or some other random piece of mail, but for her these words will stand out.

There are so many ways to receive answers that I couldn't possibly list them all. You might see a billboard on a bus or a bumper sticker on a car. You might overhear a conversation at the coffee shop, or have a book fall open in front of you at the library. From your own email inbox to the scenes of a movie that affect you, Spirit will use any means necessary to get you your answer. You will know the response is for you by the way it feels in your body. If you are receiving an answer, even the smallest detail or moment in time will have a profound effect. You will feel it in your entire body. If you don't remember ever having this experience before, just trust me on this for now—when you feel it, you will know.

Answers you live your way into

The last way of getting answers I'm going to mention is perhaps the subtlest of all. But it is also very satisfying. In addition to those profound timeless moments or the obvious direct responses, you will also receive answers—just like Rilke said—by simply living your way into them.

It's all very mysterious, but what I've discovered is that the process of asking the question alone can and does start to reshape your life. It's like you are guided very naturally, and often without even detecting it, to the actions that will resolve or provide solutions to your problem. Sometimes it is so indirect that it takes you by surprise. You might not even notice while it's happening. A few weeks or months down the line you'll look back in your journal, see a question you asked, and realize that you have already lived your way into the solution. Or possibly the answer you asked for is no longer needed or relevant because of the other solutions that have appeared in the meantime. Asking the question starts to shape your life into the answer.

As you may have noticed, none of these ways of receiving answers requires any extra work on your part. Of course there are things you need to do. When I realized I needed to move out of my house, obviously I had to start looking for another place to live. But as it turned out, someone had already mentioned to me that my friends were renting their yurt, so even that was a very obvious solution. I did the work of calling them and going over to look at it—the things a person does when they're looking for a place to live—but nothing about it was out of the ordinary. What I mean to point out here is that again, whether you are receiving it directly, experiencing it in a timeless moment, or living your way into it, the solution arrives naturally while you do the things that you would normally be doing. No extra back flips needed.

If this is all new to you, your main work will be opening yourself up to the fact that the answers are all around you. Remember, answers are to be received not tracked down. In the next chapter I will give you give you some tips that will help you recognize them more easily and use the other secret ingredient, expanded awareness. But first—you know—review.

Review

* The answers will appear in totally ordinary ways as you go about living your life. You don't have to do anything special or struggle in any way to find them.

* Anything and everything can convey an answer—from inanimate objects, events, conversations, and so on. Spirit will use any means necessary to give you your answer. All you need to do is pay attention.

* Sometimes the answers will be obvious—as in someone using the exact lan guage that you've used or directly addressing you and your question.

* And sometimes Spirit will call your attention to your answer by heighten- ing your senses. Amplified senses or a feeling of timelessness is a signal

from Spirit to you that there is something important happening that you should notice.

* You will know you're receiving a message or solution because of the way it feels in your body.

* But don't worry if you miss an answer If you need this answer, it will come up again.

* The subtlest way that answers arrive is by you living your way into them. Just asking a question starts to reshape your life into an answer. Sometimes it's so indirect that you won't even notice until later.

* Answers are to be received not tracked down. Just do what you would normally be doing—and the answer will arrive.

CHAPTER 6

Secret Ingredient #2: Expanded Awareness

In the process of writing this book, I discovered something about myself. The first person that read this book pointed out to me that what's obvious to me is not necessarily obvious to other people. You know how when you are looking out from your own eyes, everything seems quite natural and normal, but once you start talking to another person, you realize that the way you see things is very different from the way that other people look at things. To be totally honest, I wasn't entirely aware of this fact before I started working on this book. What I was writing seemed so clear to me that it took one person, and then another, and another to point out that what I was saying was actually very different from the way they were accustomed to living and looking at their lives. What was to me such an obvious and natural way of living and seeing the world was not totally evident to everyone else.

It was that feedback that prompted me to write this chapter. Now, even if you just apply what I have told you so far, your answers will come. But just like it helps to have your good friend Patience with you, there is another secret ingredient in the Getting Answers Process that helps you succeed more easily: awareness.

I want to underscore a point I made in chapter 5: anything and everything—and I do mean everything—can be used to carry a message to you. Now I want you to take this in for a moment. Look around the room that you are sitting in right now. As you do so I want you to remember that Great Spirit is not limited in any way, shape, or form. This means that every single thing—be it an inanimate object or a living breathing animal, or a circumstance that you experience—is capable of communicating great things to you. This does not mean that every single one of these things does. In most cases, that coffee mug sitting next to you is really just going to go on holding your drink! It doesn't have a secret message for you. It's not being used to give you any answers. But because Great Spirit is not limited by anything—the coffee mug *could* give you a message. One day at the very moment you say something to your aunt that you've been meaning to say for a long time, that coffee mug could fall off the table—and confirm the importance of what you've just said. Someday you may turn that mug over to put it in the dishwasher and notice that it says something on the bottom that means something to you right then. Anything is possible here.

Because Great Spirit is not limited in any way—your answers can literally come from anywhere.

Now 99% of the time, there is no message. The coffee mug is just a coffee mug. But, in order to recognize the 1% of the time that it does actually mean something, you must be open to that possibility at the start.

When I look around at my life I recognize, very easily and without trying at all, that virtually anything and everything could contain a message. Because this is a very natural way of looking at the world for me, I am never shocked when something becomes an answer. Usually, it's fun. Like the windshield wiper I mentioned moving across the window in response to my words—that was fun. When an ordinary object becomes a sign, or a person in your presence becomes a messenger, I find it very exciting!

Especially when I'm looking for answers, (and most especially if I'm hurting in any way). But honestly, even if you aren't hurting, it's good to know that Spirit is trying to communicate with you. You make it easier the moment you start to open to this knowledge. The answers are everywhere. Life can be as ordinary or as extraordinary as you choose. In order to be receptive to the answers that are all around you, you must be aware that anything could be used to communicate a message to you.

For millennia seers have known this. Without even trying, they have been able to understand the significance of even the most seemingly insignificant events in life. In his book, *The Alchemist,* Paulo Coelho calls this "looking into the soul of the world." The main character in his book learns that because we are all a part of the soul of the world, because we all come from the same essence, all aspects of the world can be used to communicate great truths. Because we are all a part of this essence, it is no surprise that anything can sometimes provide essential knowledge.

To me it looks like this: Spirit communicates with us through the ordinary because the ordinary is where we live. We all take the garbage out, prepare dinner, wash the dishes, go to work, raise our children, etc. Where else would we receive messages if not within the context of our lives? This is where we are.

Now, I've already detailed in the previous chapter some of the very obvious signals Spirit can use to get your attention, so I'm not going to go into that here. The purpose of this chapter is to open your mind to start recognizing the answers all around you, so that you'll start noticing how the events, the people, and the things in your life are pointing you in certain directions and providing answers for you.

I have a really good example, something that happened to a friend of mine. I was sitting with her one day talking about this book. She was in a bit of a funk at that moment, and in a semi-exasperated voice she said to me, "I just don't get answers like you do."

I said, "That's because you're not asking questions."

Two days later I got an email from her saying that she couldn't wait to tell me about the answers she was now getting. Simply becoming aware of the possibility had shifted everything for her.

By the time we got together, only one week later, she had four stories to tell me. Not only had she received clear advice on how to get out of her funk, she had also gotten some answers about how to better her life in general and she'd gotten information regarding a relationship issue that had been bothering her for some time. She'd never framed it as a question before; she'd never realized she could know the answer.

Some of those solutions to issues she had been wondering about, others were responses that came the moment that she became open to receiving guidance.

One of her stories beautifully illustrates the point of anything being a possible message. She said that for the past two weeks she had seen police on the road almost every time she drove and at least once a day. She noticed this; she thought it was strange. Time and time again she would be driving along and at some point a cop would pull up behind her or turn in the same direction and follow her nearly the whole way to her destination. These policemen never pulled her over, never seemed to notice her, but they were always driving on the same route she was.

The day after we spoke, she was in the car with her daughter who, when it happened again, said, "Mom! You have the worst luck!" In that moment, my friend thought, *Hey wait a minute! There is something else going on here. What is this experience trying to show me?*

She got the resounding message, *SLOW DOWN!* In becoming aware that there could be a message here, she realized that she associated the presence of these police officers with slowing down. Every time there was a cop in the area, she felt compelled to move more slowly: to drive carefully and consciously, without rushing to her destination.

What she did with that advice is something I speak about in the next chapter: Act. For now, I'll just say that applying this advice was very beneficial to her. The point of this story is that something had been occurring in her life over and over, she had noticed it, but she hadn't been aware that it was a message for her. The moment she shifted her awareness and became open to this possibility, the answer came. Sitting in the car with her daughter at her side, she had one of those profound internal moments that we have when we receive an answer. She got her, *Aha!* answer, and a message that actually improved her life.

When anything unusual or striking happens in my life I always ask myself if there is a message for me here—*Is there some deeper meaning to this particular occurrence?* Sometimes there isn't and sometimes there is. As you play with this process, and notice the answers that you receive, you will be able to perceive with more clarity which ones are answers for you and which ones are not. For now, you need only become aware of the possibility that anything and everything could be an answer.

Tips for broadening your awareness

Start to notice when something unusual occurs, or when a particular event catches your attention or happens repeatedly. This event may or may not be unusual, but you're noticing it, so ask yourself, *Is there a message for me here?* As I've said, sometimes the answer will be no—stuff does just happen—but sometimes the answer will be yes.

Here are some questions to ask yourself that will get you thinking in these terms:

— *Is there a message for me here? (This is the most direct route!)*
— *Is there another meaning behind this?*

Then, to get to the message you might ask some of the following questions:

— *What is that meaning?*
— *What was I just talking or thinking about when this thing happened?*
— *What is this moment showing me?*
— *What do I associate with this thing, person, or occurrence?*
— *What does this mean to me?*
— *Does this mean something to me in terms of my life right now?*
— *How do I feel right now in my body?*

Most often, answers will feel profound. They will have a tangible and very satisfying feeling in your body. You will discover that there is a large element of peace present. The truth always relaxes the body, and if you've asked a question that is very important for you, or that has taken you some time to formulate, you will likely feel it very strongly in your body. It's as if every pore of your body is saying, *YES!* What is most beautiful is that you will feel this resonance even if the outcome is not what you were expecting or what you wished for.

Again I want to mention that if you aren't sure—don't worry, the answer will repeat. Sometimes if you're holding on really strongly to a specific outcome—especially if it is not the one that is ultimately best for you—it can take a few times for the message letting you know what's best to get through. This was the case for me when I was wondering what to do about my living situation. When I was talking with a potential roommate and I got the first message that my answer was not to find a roommate but to move out of the house entirely, I wasn't totally sure. The truth is that I was holding on so tightly to a different conclusion that my guides were having a hard time getting through to me. They were giving me the message but because I was hoping for another, at first I didn't hear it. Nonetheless, the answer repeated until it became clear. I did get the response that I needed, the one that guided me in the best direction for my life. So Spirit will repeat until you get the information that is in line with your highest good. You can speed up the process by increasing your awareness of the way that answers are coming to you and by recognizing them as they come. In this way, when you follow through on the last step or action, you can align more quickly with your own highest good.

However, don't try too hard to find your answers. Trust me, it's easy. It really is. Once you have broadened your awareness and realize that anything could be an answer, Spirit will make it very obvious for you. You don't have to rack your brain to figure out what something means or to decipher messages. God/Presence/the Universe is very much aware of your thoughts and the associations you have with certain things. It will be obvious, or not.

About a year after I had taken the waitress position I mentioned in chapter 1, I started to have the feeling that a transition was in order. One evening when I was in back of the restaurant, I mentioned this to a friend. It was the beginning of summer, and I was describing how I didn't know if I wanted to spend all of my summer weekends serving food, how the idea of a little more freedom in my schedule seemed appealing. I wanted to go camping and do some fun summer things too.

I said, "I'm feeling ready to move on from here."

At that moment she said, "Oh, you have an ant on your hat!" and reaching up, she brushed off the ant.

Now, she couldn't have know this, but I associate ants with patience. To me the ant is the hallmark of waiting until the time is right. I notice ants often shows up in my life when I start to feel a transition coming and feel instantly ready to move on. When ants appear to me, they remind me that everything must take its due course. That I'm not to race to the finish line but to hold steady until the time is truly right.

I laughed as she removed the ant from the top of my head. Internally, I tabled my notion that I shouldn't be waiting tables for the summer, and made a mental note that my time at the restaurant would end when it was right. I didn't even mention any of this to her. She had no idea she had just delivered this message to me. But the answer was as loud as if the sky had suddenly opened up and boomed, *Aimée, be patient! The time is not right for you to leave this job yet!* As it turned out, my job did end about two months later, just as the summer was finishing. And the timing was perfect! Some dear friends of mine who live in Mexico were visiting, and I got to spend the last part of my summer attending parties and going on fun camping trips with them. I was able to make money all summer and go camping too.

The beautiful and extra special gift about broadening your awareness is that you don't always have to wait until you ask a question to receive guidance. You can, like I did in that instance, receive answers at any moment that will help guide your life for the better. Once you become aware that the answers can come from anywhere, Spirit/the Universe/Presence has a wide-open channel for communicating with you. Once you've made clear that you're open to and looking for this guidance, Spirit will send guidance whenever it can. Because I am very internally set to notice and pay attention to guidance, and because I act on it, I receive it all of the time. In many cases, this has caused me to avoid pitfalls before they even happen, or to prepare myself in advance for changes that I sensed were coming.

Once again, I want to point out that receiving answers is easy and that the solutions you receive will be relevant to you—you don't have to work hard to find the clues. Like I said, Spirit is aware of what you think. In my case Spirit knows what ants mean to me so it knew that this ant on my head would be an efficient way of communicating. If I had associated ants with, say, strength, the Universe would have not have chosen an ant to give me a message about patience. With my friend who kept seeing cops on the road, Spirit knew that, if she thought about it, she would associate seeing cops with the message *slow down*. To someone else, this could mean something entirely different. Say you have a brother who's a police officer, then for you seeing a cop might prompt you to think of your brother. You might be inspired to contact him. Someone else might associate police officers with a certain moment in their lives that taught them something. The possibilities are endless here. My point is that in communicating with you, Spirit will use whatever has meaning for you. If you do not associate police officers with your brother, the Universe will not try to get you to think of your brother by showing you a policeman!

Do you get my drift here? Don't try too hard. Just remember that anything can and may be used to send you a message or respond to your question and that Spirit will use the language and symbols that are meaningful to you when trying to get you a message. And anything and everything goes, because it is all part of your life.

Okay. We're about to move into the last critical step in receiving answers: Act. But before we do, let's review.

Review

* Spirit/God/Universe/Presence is not limited in any way, shape, or form. That means that anything and everything—any object, animal, person, or occurrence—may be used as a means to get you an answer.

* Although 99% of the time objects are just ordinary, it's easier to receive messages that 1% of the time if you are open to the fact that sometimes these ordinary objects are used to communicate with you.

* Spirit communicates with us through the ordinary because that is where we live.

* To broaden your awareness, start to notice when something unusual happens, when a particular event stands out to you, or when a circumstance keeps repeating. Then ask yourself, Is there a message for me here?

✳ Other questions you might ask yourself to get to the bottom of the meaning are these: What do I associate with this thing, person, or occurrence? What was I just talking or thinking about when this happened? Does this mean something to me in terms of my life right now?

✳ Your body is a good barometer. Many times answers will create a feeling of profound peace in your body.

✳ Remember, Spirit is aware of your thoughts and associations. It will not make you work hard to decipher messages. It will provide answers by speaking in a language that you already understand, using symbols that you already associate with certain meanings.

✳ One special bonus in broadening your awareness is that it allows you to be able to receive information on how to make your life better, sometimes before you even ask. Once Spirit/God/Presence knows you are listening and responding, it will provide you with more clues.

CHAPTER 7

Act

For some reason, people often find this to be the hardest step. The truth is there is absolutely nothing that I—or anybody, even Spirit—can do to get you to take this step. This is a decision you have to make for yourself. Spirit can and will give you all the guidance you ask for, but it is you who must act on it.

At this point, I like to remind you of the first step you took in this *Getting Answers* process. Remember at the beginning you took the time to align with the highest good. You followed the protocol and set your intention or addressed your question to your personal connection with the Divine. Consider then that is where your answers are coming from.

What this step calls for, at least at the beginning, is courage. Once you've acted on the advice a few times, you're going to discover how wonderful this makes your life. Then the final step, acting, becomes a no-brainer. Then you start acting on the guidance you get because you can see that when you've done this in the past, it's improved your life and often in ways you could never have foreseen. I've found that every time I've followed guidance, the joy this has brought me was more than I could have imagined. Countless good things happened because of it, uplifting my life in ways my small brain couldn't have dreamed. After just a few times—perhaps after just one time!—you will see that even if you don't know why at the time, following through on the answers you receive enhances your life tremendously.

When you follow the advice and guidance of Great Spirit, it's fun. It's wonderful. It's lovely. And it's good for you and not in the way that the vegetables you don't like are good for you. It's as if you've just discovered a delicious delicacy that's perfect just for you and far beyond what you would've invented on your own.

Remember when I was talking about how I found where I now live? How I heard my friend use the name of the island as I was standing in her living room? Well at the end of our conversation I said to her, "I think I need to go there." And that is what I did. I acted on the guidance I had just been given.

Keep in mind I didn't know anything about Vashon Island other than its location; and I knew that only because I had looked it up on a map. But since I had received an unmistakable signal from Spirit, and I was consciously looking for home, I felt as though I had to investigate it.

So a couple of weeks later, I got in my car and went to Vashon. The real magic began after I arrived.

As I was driving around that Saturday afternoon, the sign of this particular bar/restaurant stood out to me—I got my signal from Spirit. So in the evening, around 8 p.m., when the sign indicated there would be a band playing, I went. There was hardly anyone there and the band was still setting up, so I kept walking. I walked in the front door and right through the side door of the restaurant that led to the bar. I felt awkward. I didn't know anyone. Just hanging out alone at a bar isn't something that feels comfortable to me. If there had been some music, maybe I could have stood there, but nothing was going on yet. I didn't see anything that called my attention or caught my eye—there was no notice from Spirit—so without changing my pace at all, I headed straight out the back door of the bar. I figured at least I could reassess the situation when I got out in the fresh air—maybe come back after the band started.

Within less than 10 seconds a man with dreadlocks followed me out the door. I was just outside when he said to me, "I think you left too soon." That was a very strong message, so I turned around to face him. Then he said, "Come back in, and I'll buy you a beer—and I'm not trying to pick you up."

We stood at the counter as he bought me a beer. Then, turning around, he said, "Here I'm sure these two ladies would be happy for you to join them." He walked me over to their table and placing my drink on it he said, "Ladies, this is Aimée, she's new here, and she would like to join you." Introductions made, the man took his own beverage and went back to the game of pool he was playing.

It was, of course, all quite unusual. But I was game. Having a perfect stranger who had never seen me before follow me out the back door to tell me I had left too soon was clearly a signal I couldn't ignore. So I just made myself comfortable with the ladies. Sometime into the evening we discovered the link. I told them how I was thinking of moving here and was in town exploring the place when one of the women said, "Hey, do you want to housesit for me? We're leaving for three weeks at the end of June, and we really need someone to feed our animals while we are gone." Turns out that was the exact timing that my lease was up in Port Townsend! Of course I wanted to housesit! She was so excited to find someone to feed her four horses, two ducks, and a cat that she bought me a beer.

I joked with my mother later as I told her the story that I had walked into the place, been given a place to stay, a place to store my stuff (in her garage), and a couple of beers. I hadn't even spent a dime, and I actually found a dime on the floor!

I never saw that man again. Although I have lived here for more than four years now and been back to that bar/restaurant more times than I can count, to this day I never laid eyes on him again. I believe he was a messenger of Spirit.

Now, that was magical. And this is the kind of life you can have when you start to follow the omens and act on the messages, the signals, and the answers that come from Spirit. The gist is this: when you start to act on your answers, you start to get more. Spirit, knowing you are paying attention, will guide you as you go along.

Think of it this way: if you have a friend who is always willing to go out with you, one with whom you have a lot of fun, you're likely to make sure that she is always included in your plans. If, on the other hand, you have a friend whom you like but who constantly says no when you ask her to do something, after a while you'll stop asking her. It isn't that you enjoy her company any less; it's that she never plays, and you get tired of asking and being refused. When you start to act on the messages you get, the Universe knows you are in the game. And when you are ready and willing to play, the Universe is ready and willing to guide you to more good.

Okay, so I made the initial trip to the island and discovered a place to land when I moved. I still needed to take care of some other things before I actually got there—things like get a post office box, start scoping out housing, look around a little more. So a few weeks later I made another trip. Before I left I stopped at a friend's house to remind him to feed my cats while I was gone. As I was about to leave, he said, "You know you should contact these people I know there. I haven't seen them in years, but they are great folks. Maybe you can camp in their yard for the weekend or something." He googled them to get a current phone number, left them a message telling them I was coming for the weekend, and gave them my cell phone number.

By the time I got to the island, I had a message on my cell phone saying, "You don't have to sleep in our yard! We have a spare bedroom. You can stay as long as you like." To this day this woman and this family are among my closest friends on the island. The first week I moved here, they took me to so many parties that by the end of seven days not only had I met almost everyone who ended up being key in my life here, but I had spent so much time with them that I felt as though I'd been there forever.

As I was saying, the more you show the Universe that you are willing to act on the guidance you receive, the more support it provides. These are just a few of the true-life examples of the kind of magic that happens when you get in the habit of acting on the answers that you receive. I could give you more. In fact, I could go on and on here about how much I've loved living where I do; how the people and the place have soothed, supported, and inspired me in so many ways; how this place has felt like home to me in a way that no other place ever has… But even without all of these details, I think you get the point. It's this: Following the guidance I received brought me more joy than I could have ever imagined. I didn't have any idea what I would find when I got here, or even who was here, but I knew how to follow the guidance I got and I knew that it was leading me to something good. That is what you must learn to do too.

Follow the advice of your Highest Self, of Spirit. Act on the answers from Spirit. Acting on this advice is what gets you what you want. It produces the results you desire, the thing that prompted you to ask the question in the first place. Frankly, if you don't act on the answer, everything you've done to get it is pointless.

I did a psychic reading recently for a woman who was having a really hard time with this step. She was tuned into the messages she was getting from Spirit, but she was stuck in a fear-based paralysis (which we will address in the next chapter) and the habit from years of inertia. She was used to receiving information, but she wasn't used to acting on it. By the time she came to me, the loudest and most profound message that I was getting for her wasn't about what to do; it was simply *DO IT!!!* She already knew she needed to go to massage school; she had been receiving the signs herself. But instead of acting on it, she was sitting on the information. And not acting on it was causing her all kinds of agony. First, it kept her stuck in fear, since she never had the chance to see that following through on the advice was not going to produce the thing she feared. And second, because massage school was a necessary step in aligning this woman with her life goals, not going to massage school was crippling her soul. She was practically writhing in pain—not because she didn't know what to do but because she wouldn't do it.

Think of it this way: if you receive a message to get up and go out the door and you never do that, what happens? Nothing. Exactly nothing. That means all of the wonderful things that are waiting for you along this path never happen to you either. You don't meet the people you would've connected with, you don't receive the satisfaction of accomplishment that is waiting for you, you never get to feel the joy of this path, and you don't get the proof that the messages you hear are true. You just sit in your house wasting away in your fear and guilt, and that is not fun. I know it can be scary sometimes to take the plunge, make the leap, get out the door, go to massage school, or just do whatever it is. But if you don't act on the advice, the only person who loses is you.

In every case, acting on the answer will improve your life. That being said, however, I've noticed that some questions are more important than others and that applies to the follow-through as well. For example when I asked, *Where is my home?* I felt that this knowledge was essential for my own growth. In every part of my being I felt that I needed to be someplace else. Although I couldn't precisely name why, I knew that this was very important for my own evolution. In contrast, when I asked the question, *What other avenues would it be good for me to explore in my writing?* it didn't have the same weight. For me, that question, at that time, stemmed from a place of idle curiosity. I was just wondering. You'll know how important it is for you to act on your answer by how essential the question seems to your life. If you're asking is in response to some deep internal seeking, acting on your answer is imperative. If you're asking comes from a simple curiosity, following through will improve your life but it may not be urgent. I'll tell you, though, if you misjudge this and the answer is important to your life, Spirit will do everything it has to do to get you on course. If you try to ignore the advice, eventually the Universe will arrange matters so that you have no choice but to follow it.

Remember my friend who got the message to leave the business? Well she didn't. She wasn't ready. She wasn't yet in the habit of acting on the advice she received or understanding concretely that following those messages actually produces more joy. Instead she hung on, and she did that for months. In the end the Universe made it so that she and her partner were forced to close their establishment because business was so bad. They had to file for bankruptcy. Now I can't say for sure what would have happened if she had acted on the advice when she first got it, but my own experience has taught me that it would have likely involved a whole lot more joy than her getting into such dire financial straights that she, basically, lost everything.

Now don't worry about this. There is joy waiting for you whether you follow the guidance you receive right away or not. The Universe is not punishing you for not following through on its advice—it is simply showing you in no uncertain terms what is essential on your path to happiness. You can, by choosing to act right away, get on that happier course immediately, or you can learn the hard way that this is what you must do. The choice is yours.

I'm writing this book partially because I want you to know you can skip the painful part. You can move right to the glory if you just act. Believe me, this is something I also learned the uncomfortable way, so I know. But you don't have to do it that way. You can actually teach yourself to follow the joy by acting on the advice. Then you'll see for yourself that this option leads to good—to more pleasure and gladness than you would've imagined—and from that point on the choice will be obvious. Remember, Spirit knows more than you; it sees farther out. Spirit is leading you toward your most beneficial outcomes, both for now and later. That's what you asked for—and that's what you get!

Remember my friend who received the information about slowing down through her interaction with the police officers? Well, the very next morning she did the fourth step—she acted on the advice. Instead of rushing around her workplace in her usual manner, focusing only on the things that she needed to accomplish that day, she made the decision to consciously apply this message and take her time. As a result she struck up a conversation with one of the business's regular clients. It turned out this man—whom she saw quite frequently but had never taken the time to connect with—was in the same line of business that she was and had been doing it for a lot longer. He had list of connections and whole lot of knowledge that she didn't have. As they stood there chatting, he easily and freely shared tips and advice with her. He gave her the names of people to talk to and also recommended certain approaches for some of them. Now, this was valuable information! It actually made her life easier. And it was knowledge that she would never have garnered if she hadn't acted on the message that she had received the day before. In fact this man had been coming into her workplace for months, but because of her usual internal drive and motivation to focus on getting things accomplished, or going quickly to the next destination, she had failed to access the help available to her.

Here is another extremely simple analogy. Of course, this doesn't necessarily mirror in complexity the questions and answers you will receive, but it's clear so I'm going to use it anyway to make a point. Say you are standing in your house feeling stinky and miserable. You get the message that taking a bath will make you feel loads better. However, even though you received the solution, you don't take a bath. Where does that leave you? Yep: Stinky and miserable. That's right. And you know what, you're likely to grow ever more stinky and miserable until you do something about it! So, ACT! Do it! Trust the Universe! It really is the best thing!

Take it from me, the more often you just do this, the less courage it takes. After a while it becomes as automatic as breathing. When your experience shows you time and time again that acting on the answers you receive brings you good, and that the Universe will guide you as you go along, then whenever you hear the responses, you just do it. If you are not at that point yet, use my experience. I've been asking for, receiving, and acting on the guidance I get for years. I know it works. You'll have that same experience once you start to follow through. All you need to do is do it! Why? Because doing it is going to make your life better. You might not know exactly how, or in what way, but you'll see—it'll be good.

Review

---

* Nobody but you, not even Spirit, can make the decision to act on the advice that you receive. It is a choice you must make for yourself.

* Remember you took the time to align with the highest good, so you know this is where your answers are coming from.

* Acting on your answer takes courage but only at first.

* The more you act on the advice that you receive the more acting becomes a no-brainer. Your experience will show you that following through on this advice actually does enhance your life in ways you often could not have even imagined.

* Once you act on your answers, you start to get more. Spirit, knowing you are paying attention, will give you more guidance as you go along.

* Acting on your messages gets you results; it produces the thing you wanted. Not acting on your messages makes getting the messages pointless.

* Because you've aligned with the highest good, the answers you receive always add to, enhance, or improve your life. To receive this benefit, however, you have to act on the answers.

* There's nothing like your own experience to show you this, but before you have that, you can use mine. I've been getting—and acting on—answers for years with positive results. I know it works.

* Now, just do it!

CHAPTER 8

Secret Ingredient #3: Fear Transformed

I've included this chapter because I want to be up front about the fact that even if your answer comes from the highest place, you may still experience fear when you go to act on it, or even when you *think* about acting on it. Fear may come up, but do not take this as a sign that you're on the wrong track. The only thing that fear indicates for certain is that your heart is still beating (probably rapidly), and you are still breathing in and out (probably very shallowly). The problem is not that we experience fear; the problem is when we allow that fear either to paralyze us or to dictate our actions.

In this chapter I will address some ways you can look at and understand fear so that you can avoid letting it control you. I'll also give you a few tricks for transforming fear when it does come up.

Fear doesn't necessarily indicate that something is threatening

Like most humans, I've experienced fear so many times in my life when it was not warranted that I could probably give hundreds of examples here. The one I am choosing to describe is something that happened recently.

Not too long ago I taught a weekend workshop on *Getting Answers.* Because my neighbor suggested this workshop to me—I spoke about it in chapter 5—and so, from its very inception, I felt that it was Spirit inspired. I wasn't nervous in preparing for it. I knew I wanted to teach the *Getting Answers* formula, and that my role would include being "the oracle" and giving readings to our students. I felt comfortable with both of these activities and had been doing for some time. I was co-teaching the workshop with another woman and, although we had just met, I trusted her knowledge and ideas. Even during the planning stages there was a synergy between us that I was excited about. I could tell that we were about to create something that would be really worthwhile for both our students and ourselves. The planning had gone off without a hitch and even the first evening went beautifully.

Then on the second morning of our workshop, the morning that I would start my work doing readings, I became overwhelmed by fear. I couldn't tell how much of it was my own, and how much of it was the feelings I was picking up from the students. After all, each person there was about to receive an intuitive reading in front of a group of virtual strangers. Although I knew that I would not get any information that would be unbeneficial for them to receive in this setting, I could see how someone not familiar with this process could be afraid. Regardless of where the fear was coming from, I felt it in my body. I felt petrified. That morning prior to class I had done all of my usual tricks to get centered—namely, going for a run and meditating. Still when we started class my heart was beating so fast I felt the pulse and strength of it might actually lift up my shirt. Luckily, I had to go on. And I did. Even though my heart was racing, my palms were sweating, and I could barely even feel my own legs, I moved forward. And guess what happened? It went perfectly! As soon as I started the first reading, I felt myself relax into the ease of what I do. I lost the fear altogether. By the end of that reading, my breathing and heart rates were totally back to normal. I lost the feeling of being under the siege of fear, and instead I felt thrilled.

I learned from this experience. It was so profound that I remembered it. The next time I felt this type of heart racing fear I was driving down the road. I don't remember what I was thinking about that caused me to start panicking, but it didn't take me long to wise up. *Wait a minute,* I said to myself, *I know this feeling! This is the exact feeling that I had before the start of my workshop and look what happened there! It was a great weekend. Everything went off without a hitch, and even the student evaluations showed that everyone loved it.*

Right then and there I decided that experience had taught me that I could override this feeling. The feeling wasn't warranted. *I'm not going to believe this fearful story,* I told myself. *It's all bull.* You know what happened? My body quieted down. Just like it had when I finally got down to doing my work in the workshop, my body relaxed. Apparently it just needed a reminder from me: *We are not under siege. Our life is not on the line here. We are going to be okay.* And presto. Ahhh! It was liberating to realize once again that I don't have to believe everything I think!

So, first and foremost, recognize that experiencing fear does not necessarily indicate that something is truly scary.

Fear is unavoidable

You might as well just accept right off the bat that fear is an unavoidable sensation. Being human is enough to assure that you will experience fear from time to time. We are biologically programmed to feel fear. I like to think of it as a throw back to the days when saber tooth tigers could be looming around the next bush. This helps me remember that, at its core, fear is a warning mechanism designed to ensure my safety. Now, however, in the 21st century, the things that cause us fear have very little chance of causing our death. Face it, even though your heart may be beating at a rate you could hardly calculate, your hands might be shaking, and your palms might be sweating, that thing that you are afraid of is not really going to kill you. Teaching that class, talking to that person, taking that job is not going to cost you your life. Even if it seems like it, the truth is that your boss (co-worker, friend, etc.) is not literally going to open their jaws and bite off your head. If you speak your truth, you are still going to be okay.

Although fear is a natural human experience that we may not be able to control having, we do have control over whether or not we let fear dictate our actions.

One of the most profound lessons that I learned about fear came up one day while I was hiking in the Colorado Rockies. I was standing in the woods by myself eating a hard-boiled egg when three ptarmigan birds approached. They stood there watching as the crumbs fell from my hands, and before long they began to go for them. Gathering courage, they were soon snatching up crumbs practically off of my feet.

Their brazenness made me think they might even eat out of my hand. So I put some crumbs in my right palm and held it out. In a matter of moments a grey and white bird was flying straight at me. My heart beat so quickly that at the last second I jerked my hand away. Three times this happened. I was afraid--actually, I was petrified. Visions of puncture wounds from bird claws flashed through my mind. I saw the gaping hole that the beak was sure to leave in my palm as it grabbed the egg white. I wondered, *Will I ever be able to use that hand again? What do I have in the car that I might wrap my wound in as I drive myself to the hospital?"*

These thoughts were going through my mind and blood was racing through my veins, when it dawned on me that my own fear was robbing me of what could be one of the most amazing experiences of my life—having wild birds come to me and eat right out of my hand. *Am I going to let my own fear deprive me of this experience?* I asked myself. Just then, the words of my meditation teacher flash through my mind. She said, "A yogi is not one who does not experience fear, but rather one who stares fear in the face and watches it back down."

I decided right then and there that I would not let fear destroy this moment. And I decided to get out and put on the thin gloves that I had in my glove box! Planting my feet on the ground, and taking a deep breath, I held out my arm with the glove and egg crumbs and stared straight ahead. The bird flew at me again and landed to grab the crumbs. For fifteen minutes the birds landed on my hand, staying longer each time. They began to eat standing on my (now ungloved) palm, not even bothering to fly away to swallow their treat. They were so gentle, perching effortlessly and pecking the crumbs without even grazing my palm. By the end they were perching two at a time, silently taking in long drinks of my appearance. I was elated! Standing in the middle of the forest looking into the eyes of wild birds perched on my own outstretched hand was an unbelievable experience.

It continued. A few hours later, as I packed up, I returned to the same spot, and opened my empty hand. Almost immediately the birds answered my call, their soft feathery touch alighting on my palm. Beady eyes met human eyes once more as we watched each other for several long moments. It was an experience I will never forget, one I come back to again and again as I think about and experience fear. It showed me the kind of magic that is waiting for me when I override my fear. And it taught me what fear most often indicates—it's a launch into the unknown.

Fear indicates you're heading into unknown territory

In a concrete way, that experience in the woods taught me that fear comes up not in response to something that is truly threatening but as an almost automatic reaction to moving into unknown territory. In truth the birds were not a hazard to me. Their beaks and claws were gentle beyond my expectations. The fears came from my mind, which, recognizing that I was moving into completely unfamiliar terrain, started circling through the list of possible outcomes and highlighting all of the negative ones, just so I would know. This is normal. This is what fear does. This is what that warning mechanism is really for. Rather than being a means of paralyzing you, fear signals you are moving into something new.

In the case of your questions and answers, experiencing fear may actually be a good sign. It indicates you are about to do something that you have never done before. Clearly if the status quo had been working, you wouldn't have been asking for a new solution. So the way I see it, if you are about to try something new—that is a good sign.

So, learn to recognize fear not as a sign that you should stop in your tracks, but as a simple signal from your body that you are moving into new territory. Just because your mind runs through every negative outcome doesn't mean these things will actually happen. Fear's presence is more like a biological alert system. It's giving you the message to stay alert and present—notifying you that you are about to enter new terrain, or make new tracks. This is not dangerous; it's just unknown.

When you think about it, you have already entered into new territory thousands of times in your life, and you're still breathing. This moment will likely not be any different.

Fear is all in your mind

The truth is—it's all in your mind. When I was afraid while driving down the road the other day, it was all in my mind. The state of panic elicited in my body had nothing to do with my being behind the wheel. Likewise, the hand-eating birds—a figment of my active imagination. The next time you experience fear, take a look around you and become aware of what is happening at that moment. Are you driving your car, lying in your bed, sitting on your couch? Is anything truly scary happening right now? I can almost guarantee the answer will be no. Really, you're fine. You're just lying in bed worrying, drawing a bowl of worst case scenarios from a stew of infinite possibilities. Well, stop it. Recognize that nothing is scarier than those thoughts. Even the experience itself will be less frightening than the frantic thoughts you're having about it. Especially when that experience involves applying the advice you've been given, and acting on your answer. So remember—it's all in your mind. That's where the fear starts, and that is where you can end it.

Tricks for transforming fear

This check-list has all of my best advice for overcoming fear.

* **OVERRIDE FEAR; DON'T LET IT STOP YOU**—The best way I've found of dissipating fear is to do the thing that you know you must. In some cases, as with the class I had to teach, you will be forced to override your fear. I mean, I suppose I could have just copped out on the class, but that was never really an option for me. But sometimes you will be all alone, as I was with the birds, and no one but you will make you do it. That day in the Colorado forest, I could have walked away from that experience—and completely missed the magic. Thank God I did not. There will be many times when you too will have the chance to walk away. Don't. Fear looms huge. It can pretty much take over every other emotion you experience, and shade everything you do, but there is another quality to fear—it has the ability to dissipate immediately. You only see this once you do the thing you must do. Then, poof, like smoke after the fire has been put out, fear disappears. It's almost like fear was never there. The moment you take action, or do the thing you are afraid of, you find out all those scary ideas were just a bunch of baloney. With those "what if" warnings obviously superfluous, fear just simply vanishes. Gone.

* **RECOGNIZE THE PHYSICAL SIGNS**—Increased heart beat, shallow breathing, panicked thinking, sweaty palms, shaky hands, taut body, hunched shoulders—you are afraid. Translation—you are entering into the unknown. This is your moment to recognize fear, look it in the face, and

watch it back down. If you want, you can thank fear as it heads out. It did, after all, give you the clever warning signal that you are about to do something you've never done before. Thanks for the heads up. Now, bye-bye.

* **IDENTIFY FEARFUL THOUGHTS**—Do you feel frantic to do something, anything? Do you hear yourself thinking about all of the bad things that could happen to you if you move forward on said thing? Do you find yourself creating wonderfully horrific futures for yourself in your mind? Fearful thoughts are negative, frantic, and inconsistent. One day they tell you that you can't because of this, the next day they tell you that you can't because of that. Is this good advice? No. Do not heed these frantic thoughts. Acknowledge these thoughts, but do not act on them. This is just fear doing what it does—warning you of every possible scenario, giving you a head's up on every worst case. These are not your cases. You are acting on your answer, which will bring you good.

* **GET PERSPECTIVE**—Think about it. In all cases whatever is bothering or frightening you is not going to last forever. You are not going to spend the rest of your life worrying about said thing. You absolutely will not be stuck in this experience. The shaking of your hands will pass, your heart will also eventually calm, and you will be able to feel your body again. So take heart. No matter how huge your fear seems right now, there is going to come a time in your life when you won't even remember this moment. How many times has this already happened to you? Personally, I can't even count them. Sometimes fear just takes time to dissolve. Wait it out. It will end.

* **USE YOUR BREATH**—Breathing is one of the most affective ways to affect what is happening in your body. If you feel calm and relaxed you naturally breathe more deeply. The moment that you are stressed and afraid your breathing becomes very shallow. Try using your breath to regulate your emotions. Give your body the message that everything is okay by inhaling deeply. If you start to do this regularly when you experience fear, it will become an automatic calming reaction to fear.

✳ **EXERCISE**—Exercise is good for so many things. But I've noticed especially during times of stress, it is a great way to keep anxiety from lodging in the body. I run it out. If you are feeling particularly fearful, try going for a run yourself. It worked for our ancestors. Even if you just run break-neck speed down the street for a few moments, it will help. What's especially effective is setting the intention before you start to release your body of any excess and unwanted fear or anxiety.

✳ **TELL YOUR FRIENDS**—Another good way I've discovered of dissipating fear is to tell my friends about it. Oftentimes, the moment you vocalize your fear, you realize how ridiculous it is. Either that, or they will. I was talking to my friend Dana not too long ago when I told her about this great fear of mine. I wish I could remember what I actually said, but I can't because the fear is gone now. It dissipated because of Dana's reaction. She was silent for a moment and then she said, "I'm sorry but when you say that I can't help but want to burst out laughing!" Of course I started laughing too. When your friends laugh at something you're afraid of, you can take it as a sign that it is a totally bogus fear. Even if they don't laugh—or you don't—you'll find that speaking your fears has the profound effect of releasing them from your body. It frees you from carrying that fear inside, and like your breath on the wind, it disappears.

✳ **FIND A ROLE MODEL**—Now I know she's a character from fiction, but one of my favorite models of fearlessness is J.K. Rowling's Luna Lovegood. Just watch the 5th Harry Potter movie, Order of the Phoenix, and you'll know what I'm talking about. There is a scene where Harry and his gang are wandering the halls of the Ministry of Magic. It's the middle of the night. They've broken in. And as far as you can tell, they may be about to face the Dark Lord himself—or at least his henchmen. These are the wicked wizards responsible for the torture and murder of several sets of parents among Harry's crew. They are not the sort of people you would wish to see on the street in daylight, let alone in the middle of the night virtually on your own. What is Luna Lovegood's reaction? She looks like she's wandering the halls of an amusement park. The underlying emotions betrayed on her face are amazement and curiosity. Fiction or not, I was truly inspired by this. Watching someone in the face of possibly imminent death not immobilized put my life into a whole different perspective! This character is so at home with the mysterious, so accustomed to the unknown, that it doesn't even occur to her to be afraid.

Now, answer this for me: who is more likely to succeed in any given situation?

A. a calm person

B. a frantic fearful person

The answer—and please notice that this is the only answer I'm giving you in the whole book: A.

Okay—so, it doesn't have to be Luna Lovegood. It could be Mahatma Gandhi, your six year-old daughter, or any inspiring person of your choice. But locking onto a role model you feel has been particularly un-thwarted by fear is a good way to help yourself transform your own fear. If you have to, the next time you experience a panicked thought, pretend you are that person—become your own role model of fearlessness.

The motto is this: Fear happens, don't let it control you. You may not have a choice about whether or not you become afraid from time to time, but you do have a choice in what you do about it. Remember, we're talking about your answer here— the one sent to you straight from the Highest Good. Overrule that fear. You can trust your answer, but you can not trust fear.

Next we're going to move on to helping you refine your attitude so that you can get the most from this process. But before we do that, let's review.

Review

---

* Experiencing fear is not a sign that you are on the wrong track. It is a sign that your heart is still beating, and you're still breathing in and out.

* The existence of fear does not necessarily mean that something is scary. If you look at your own life I'm sure you'll see examples of times you were afraid when the situation did not warrant it.

* Fear is unavoidable. You will likely experience it from time to time. Accept it, but do not let it control you.

* Fear is a biologically programmed warning mechanism. The problem is that in this day and age fear rarely signals something that is truly life threatening.

* More than anything, fear signals your entrance into the unknown. That's okay. Clearly you needed to do something differently or you wouldn't have been asking for an answer.

* Fear is all in your mind. It's like a movie that your mind is creating. Get out of the horror scenes and back to reality. Probably nothing scary is actually happening right now.

* The best way to stop fear dead in its tracks is to do the thing you know you must. Fear can't help but depart once it sees that all of the stuff it dreamed up doesn't happen.

* Recognize the physical signs of fear. Thank them for notifying you that you are now entering new territory.

* Identify your fearful thoughts. They have a frantic and inconsistent quality. Do not act on these thoughts—that's just fear running through every possible scenario.

* Get perspective. The truth is you will not be afraid of this whatever-it-is your whole life. Sometimes fear just needs time to dissolve naturally.

* Use your breath. Taking deep breaths gives the body the signal that everything is going to be fine.

* Exercise. Running is particularly good for getting rid of fear. Sprint down the road if you need to, it's what your ancestors did.

* Reveal your deepest fears to your friends. It releases them from your body— and sometime even becomes something to laugh about.

* Find a role model of fearlessness. The next time you are afraid, pretend you are that person.

Remember in the end, we are talking about your answer here. It's a solution that is in alignment with your own highest good. Really and truly, it's only going to add to your life in a positive way.

CHAPTER 9

Secret Ingredient # 4: A Positive Attitude

Like all of the other secret ingredients, the last, a positive attitude, is not totally necessary to your getting answers. You can choose to be as grumpy as you want. You will still get answers. However, I've noticed that the crabbier a person is, the less likely they are to actually recognize the answers when they appear. They are so busy thinking about how life sucks, that they don't have time to notice the answer to their problem is practically hitting them in the face. This is why I included positive attitude as the last secret ingredient. It also makes the journey that much more enjoyable.

When we're waiting for our answer, or waiting for circumstances to line up, or if something that we perceive as undesirable is happening, it can be hard to keep a positive attitude. Sometimes your mood can take a dive if the thing that you want most isn't happening yet, or if you just know that what is happening is not what you want. This chapter is intended to remind you of some key things about your attitude that will help to bolster you when you get in those situations.

You may not have thought about it in these terms before, but in any and every moment choosing your attitude is both your greatest freedom and your greatest power. One of my role models for this is Nelson Mandela. He spent 27 years in a prison cell, and still he came out not hating his captors and, instead, wondering how they could work together. Think about this—nearly 30 years in a cell. Chances are whatever is happening to you right now has not been going on for that long. There's an even better chance that you're not confined in an eight-by-eight foot concrete cell. I'm sure Nelson Mandela had bad days, but if he could manage to keep his attitude positive enough to lead him to a presidency, I'm sure I can maintain my attitude when things are not going the way I would like in my own life. No matter what is happening in your life, the choosing of your attitude is a decision and power that lies strictly and always in your hands. It is a liberty that can never be denied you or taken away.

Sometimes in life we don't have a choice about things. Stuff happens, right? Someone rear-ends your car, you lose your job, your girlfriend breaks up with you, you lose sleep for three nights in a row because your neighbor's dog won't stop barking. Real, serious, and unforeseeable stuff happens in life. That is part of the journey, part of the drama. However, in any one of those cases, you have a choice to dwell on the negative or to search out and sustain yourself on the positive.

I am by no means talking about stifling grief or hurt. I am merely pointing out that in any situation you have the opportunity to choose your outlook. Once I got a call from a friend who was going through a rough time and said that she was giving herself 24 hours to have a "pity party." That's right. For that period of time she was allowing herself to feel as pitiful and sorrowful as she wanted, without any judgment. But when that time was up, she was going to buck up, seek the positives of the situation, figure out what she needed to do given the circumstances, and then do it. It was that simple. I loved her idea of giving herself a timeline. I mean you don't want to suppress true sadness, if that is what you're feeling. But you also don't want to get stuck in that place, or live your life from that dreary viewpoint. At a certain point you need to take responsibility for choosing your attitude. If only for the simple reason that a positive outlook makes you feel better, that's the one to choose.

Determining the perspective you are going to take is akin to choosing the type of life you are going to lead. Opting for a positive position says you choose the joyful life. In any situation you have the option to watch through a beautiful, clear, colorful light or through a dark, filmy, sooty filter. It's like the difference between admiring a beautiful stained glass window, and trying to peer through filthy, cruddy, blackened glass. It's really that simple. Either way will shape the quality of your life and how you feel. The truth is that just as you are likely to experience fear at one point or another, you are also likely to come across situations that you wish were otherwise. Sometimes the only choice you have in the matter is how you choose to see it. Choosing a positive point of view is making the statement, *I choose to have a good life, even in a less than desirable situation.*

When I think of this topic, two stories or quotes come to my mind. The first is from the movie, *Seven Years in Tibet.* In the movie, the Dalai Lama says to the main character, "We have a saying in Tibet. If the problem can be solved, there is no use worrying about it. If it can't be solved, worrying will do no good."

There is a great parable I've heard and read many times in other places. It is about a Cherokee elder telling his grandson about the forces that lie in each person. He describes this as the battle between two wolves that live within us all.

"One is unhappiness," he says. "It's fear, worry, anger, jealousy, sorrow, self-pity, resentment, and inferiority. The other is Happiness. It is joy, love, hope, serenity, kindness, generosity, truth, and compassion."

The youngster thinks about this for a minute and then he asks his grandfather, "Which wolf wins?"

The old Cherokee replies, "The one you feed."

Your attitude shapes your life. Your attitude affects your choices, and your choices determine your destiny. Even on the most basic level this is easy to see. If you're in a bad mood, how do you generally react to the people and circumstances around you? Sourly. How do you view what is happening to you? Badly. Your mood defines how you experience this world. If the same circumstance were to happen to two people, the one in a negative mind frame is likely to scowl and complain while the one feeling buoyant and joyful may just shrug and smile. Everything depends on your point of view and on how you choose to see the situation.

I'm not saying that it's necessarily going to be easy, especially if you are in the habit of being negative. But here's the thing: choosing to be happy is like learning to drive a car. At first taking on this new skill is really hard. You don't have any idea what you're doing. You are struggling to keep the car going, while pushing in the clutch and changing gears, not to even mention managing the steering wheel. Like anything in life, it takes practice. But once you get the hang of it, you can drive a car with very little effort. It comes to you automatically: you recognize that it's time to shift your car from 3rd to 4th gear; you know how to turn the wheel in the direction you want to go. Of course you must do the shifting, you turn the wheel, but you don't have to sit there and figure out how to do it. And in every moment you have a choice. You decide which way to steer the car. The moment you recognize that you are veering off course, or driving your car headlong into a storm, you can choose to turn it in a different direction. You can decide to take the sunny scenic route. Even if your ultimate destination is beyond your control, you can choose which way to get there.

Sometimes for me it comes down to some very clear and simple questions: *What makes me feel better? How would I prefer to feel right now?* When I find I'm standing in the rain, here are a few of the tricks I use to get myself back on the sunny side of life.

Get a good night's sleep

Or better yet, get several. Going to bed early is one of the easiest and most effective ways that I know of to shift my mental attitude. It sounds ridiculously simple, and it is, but getting to sleep well before midnight for at least one night or, better yet, three nights in a row is one of the best methods I know of to reset your internal everything. If your attitude needs an adjustment, try it. If you're feeling stressed and overwhelmed, just get some sleep. You'll probably be surprised at what a huge difference this commonplace adjustment can make. Sometime after I noted the strong affect that an early bedtime had on me, I came across some literature that said that, according to Chinese medicine, every hour you sleep before midnight is equal to two after midnight.

Time and time again I've been amazed at how getting in bed as early as possible (ideally before 10 p.m.) a few nights in a row can shift everything. The fog lifts, the day brightens, and anxious feelings just melt away. If you're looking for an easy fix to your attitude, this is one of the simplest I know.

Focus on what you are thankful for

There is nothing like a good dose of gratitude to get you out of negative rut. I like to remember this saying I once heard: "A wise person counts her blessings, a fool counts her misfortunes." I don't care who you are or what is happening in your life, I know for certain that in all of it there is something to be grateful for. In the most difficult circumstance, there is always some benefit. Shifting your focus to what is good about the situation gets your focus off of what's bad about the situation. Make a list. At the top of your page write, "I am so grateful that…" and challenge yourself to come up with all of the good you can. Another way to do this is to start asking questions like these: *What good is coming out of this situation? What am I thankful for right now?*

My favorite passage on gratitude comes from Wallace Wattles: "Gratitude brings your whole mind into closer harmonies with the creative energies of the universe." Now if that's not a reason to change the negative thinking into something grateful and positive, I don't know what is. Not only does it make you feel better, it makes you more likely to attract good things and it keeps you connected with Source. The creative energies of the Universe (or your version of the Divine) are exactly what you're relying upon to get your answer! Gratitude connects you with your own power to create good in your life.

Remember what it feels like to be loved

I notice that with some people, when I'm around them I truly light up. I'm not sure exactly why; there may be many reasons and these may be different, depending on the person. One thing I know is that this is an experience that I generate in my own body. Another thing I know is that when I have this on-top-of-the-world feeling, everything I do is not only okay, it's great. I have become a shining light of a person, and it is I who have generated that feeling in my body. So, next time you are feeling in the dumps, remember what it feels like to be in the presence of someone you love, someone who loves you back. Remember that nothing, except your own mood, has changed from that moment to this one. You are still the same loveable creature you were in their presence. That light you shine then belongs to no one but you.

I remember a time I was going to meet this guy for a date. It was a new relationship, practically a first date, and I felt awkward and nervous. The place that I was meeting this guy was just around the corner from a shop a friend of mine owned. On a whim, as I was walking by my friend's shop, I decided to just pop in and say a quick hello before I met up with my date. Just a few minutes in the presence of someone who knew and loved me completely shifted my energy. By the time that I met the man a few minutes later, I had returned to my confident self, at home in my own skin and with who I am. Of course it's not always that convenient; a friend of yours may not just happen to be nearby when you're feeling awkward. However, you can always remember that friend, bring them into your mind. You can remember the way they see you, the way that you feel in their presence. You can remind yourself that you are loveable and loved, and that no matter what else is happening in your life, this is true.

Remember that everything is working out for the best

Sometimes this is hard to remember, but fundamentally I believe it to be true. Just because in this moment you don't know why this may be doesn't mean that it doesn't fit into some grand plan that really is working out for the best.

I had my own lesson in this just a few weeks ago. It was 4:00 a.m., and I was on my way to the airport. Actually, since I live on an island, I was on my way to the ferry. Once on the mainland I had opted to take the bus to the airport since I neither wanted to drive my car to the airport, nor pay for a week's worth of parking. The combination of both the early flight, and the bus schedule had me leaving on a 4:30 a.m. ferry. When I got off the boat I was going to have to wait out in the cold for about 45 minutes to catch the bus that would take me there. I was fine with all of this. It was inconvenient but not horrible. The problem came on my way to the ferry. I was driving down the road at 3:45 a.m. racing to catch the boat when I realized that I had forgotten my cell phone. Now I have to say that I'm usually never awake at this time of day, and despite the fact that I was actually driving my car, for the most part my body and definitely my mind, were barely aware that I wasn't still sleeping. I continued to drive forward, though a bit more slowly now, as I calculated what this would mean to my trip. Could I survive for the next ten days without my cell phone? I know that people used to exist without cell phones, but all of the contact information for every single person I was going to see was in that phone. Some of them weren't even in the phone book. Without the phone I would have no way of contacting some of the very people that I was flying all the way out to visit. I absolutely had to get the phone. So I did.

I had the mission accomplished and phone in hand heading back toward the ferry dock when I started to contemplate the ramifications of this event. I knew I could still make my flight, but by this point I had missed the early boat, and therefore the bus I needed. In the chill 4:00 a.m. air my mind immediately started to spin out of control. It was creating all of these horrible scenarios about having to drive to the airport and pay as much in parking as I had for the plane ticket. (It had been a great deal.)

I was in 4:00 a.m. hell, working myself into a panic, when I had this dawning moment of clarity. I realized that according to my general life belief, everything is always working out for the best. If that is the case, then this little 4:00 a.m. glitch which included the unusual circumstance of me not only forgetting my cell phone, but also of me forgetting to look at the reminder note about the cell phone, had to be no different. I used my breath techniques to calm my sleep-deprived nerves and I told myself that this circumstance was no different.

By the time I got to the ferry dock, I felt at ease, certain that even if I never knew what the reason was, this couldn't be the one and only exception to my belief. Guess what happened? The first woman I talked to told me that she had been here in time for the 4:30 a.m. boat but that it hadn't arrived. The second person I talked to was going to the airport and offered to give me a ride. I laughed to myself as I got in the car. Not only did I not have to drive but, in terms of money, I didn't have to pay for parking or take a cab, and I ended up saving even the $2.50 I would have spent on the bus. I also didn't have to wait for the bus for 45 minutes in the cold. I got a ride to the airport with a nice gentleman who had been visiting his son on the island, and we talked about the Getting Answers process the whole way.

On that same trip I bought a card that says, "What if you just knew that everything was working out perfectly?" I have it hanging in my kitchen now and to see it still makes me smile. So when things aren't going exactly how you planned, or not even how you would like, try looking at it this way—things are actually working out in the best way possible. Maybe the thing that looks like a catastrophe now is leading you toward something even better. Nelson Mandela's story is another great example of this. To me, his life also reminds me that just because things suck right now doesn't mean you aren't headed for greatness. Even from the worst situations, benefits beyond your wildest dreams can come. I don't mean to imply that there are not tragedies in this life or that you could never be in a dangerous situation. There are, and you could. But I've observed that what we often become fixated on is not the reality that's before us but the embellishments and interpretations we create in our own minds. Even in the very worst life dramas, we can take better care of ourselves, and everyone else, by focusing our attention on what's positive.

Use humor—see yourself as a character in a movie

One of my favorite things to do to trip myself back into a positive attitude is to see myself as a character in a movie—especially if things are going badly or I'm experiencing a string of less than inspiring events. In response, I start to view myself as a heroine in a comedy. You know, woman runs up against one ridiculous challenge after another and of course conquers them all in a dramatic and comedic way. I tried this recently when I discovered that I had to chop a whole cord of wood on my own. When the pile of wood was delivered, I actually cried. It was so overwhelming. Not only did I have to stack it all alone, which would have been daunting but still okay, I also had to chop a huge portion of it. Instead of delivering the wood in the specifications that I required—lengths and widths that would fit my wood-burning stove—the man delivered a whole cord of wood that was too big.

Since I don't have a tape measure, I had to cut a string—a lavender ribbon to be exact—that was the length of my stove. Then I had to go out to the pile and measure every single piece of wood against my lavender ribbon to determine whether or not it would fit in my stove. Slowly, I separated the mountain of wood into two piles: wood that was too long and wood that was too thick. Anyway, imagine a woman alone, whose only source of heat is wood, standing next to an enormous pile of wood almost as tall as she is and three times in length, most of which will not even fit in her stove. It's not so funny—at least it wasn't to me. However, when you see this same woman, tackling the pile with her work gloves and her lavender satin measuring ribbon, you can't help but think it's ridiculous. At least I couldn't. In my mind I saw myself in contrast to my neighbors, all snug in their electrically heated homes, and it just got even funnier. What I was doing, and my life just seemed so absurd that I couldn't help but laugh. The medicine worked. I wasn't exactly thinking, *Yeah, bring on the wood!* but I wasn't crying over it either!

Use affirmations

The messages that you tell yourself actually create your life. In truth, they dictate how you live and what you choose to see and experience. You can decide to give yourself positive and uplifting messages that will make your life magic rather than tragic. The possibilities are endless, but here are a few of the ones I use:

— *The Universe (God, Source, Creator) is looking out for me.*
— *Spirit has my best interest in mind.*
— *My life is simple and easy.*
— *Answers come to me often.*
— *Everything is working out for the best.*
— *I am, at all times, being guided to the best possible life for me.*

For even more punch, try turning these statements into questions. Your brain will automatically start giving you the answers.

The truth is that you have the ability to write yourself into any story you want. Choose to be the funny, fun, loveable, grateful, inspired hero or heroine in the play of your life. If you remember your power and freedom to do so, you can never go wrong, and you'll enjoy the ride.

Review

* The ability you have to choose your attitude is both your greatest freedom and your greatest power.

* This is a liberty that can never be taken from you. You can't always control what life gives you and sometimes you can't even control exactly where you are going, but you always have a choice as to the attitude that you bring along for the ride.

* If you can do nothing else, choose to look on the positive side simply because it makes you feel better. Hel-lo? That's a no-brainer!

* Choosing to see the bright side of things takes practice. It's like learning to drive a car. With a bit of practice you'll do it automatically.

* Get a good night's sleep—or better yet get several. It's one of the easiest and most effective ways to change your mood for the better.

* Find things to be grateful for. Gratitude gets your mind off what isn't working, and it also aligns you with Source.

* Remember what it feels like to be loved. That shining person you are in the presence of someone who loves you is the same person you are right now.

* Remember life is always working out for the best, even when you can't see why or where things will end up.

* Use humor: even tragedy can be comedy with the right shift in perspective. See yourself as the hero or heroine in a comedy where you dramatically and hilariously rise to the challenge of your absurd life!

* The messages you give yourself actually create your experience of life. So use uplifting positive thoughts and affirmations to remind yourself that the Universe truly is on your side.

CHAPTER 10

The *Getting Answers* Checklist

Are you stuck? You can go through this handy list of reminders—a short course that covers the entire *Getting Answers* process.

* Before asking your question, did you align with the Highest? Specifically, did you make a personal intention statement? (It would be something akin to this: *I only receive answers that are in line with my highest good.*) Or, have you addressed your question to your personal connection with the Divine?

* Did you ask a question? In other words, did you state what you're looking for, missing, or wishing to know as a question? And are you writing it down or repeating it to yourself?

* Does that question express what you really want to know? It's possible you feel dissatisfied because your question or answer doesn't reflect what you truly need at this moment. Do some self-inquiry. Chapter 3 has some starter questions. Ask yourself questions until you discover a question you don't know the answer to... or one that helps you understand what you need or want right now. Then, you can ask how to get it.

✳ Are you taking advantage of your old friend Patience? Sit in the room with her. Let her stroke your hand. Even if you don't know this, she knows your answer is coming.

✳ Are you recognizing your answers? Spirit/God/ the Universe is not limited in any way, and that means that anything and everything can be used as a means to get your answer to you. Messages are often "ordinary"—they show up within the context of your life because that is where you live. Use some of the tips in chapter 6 to help you expand your awareness and ensure that you aren't missing a message that is right in front of you.

✳ Have you received your answer but failed to act on it? Do it! Do the thing that you know you must do. Remember, it truly will bring you joy. As soon as you try it, you'll find out.

✳ Are you stuck in fear? Being fearful happens to the best of us. You can feel fear without letting it control you. Remember, most of the time experiencing fear doesn't indicate that anything is actually threatening you. The feeling will pass. Use some of the transforming fear techniques of chapter 8 to get out of fear, or just wait it out. Trust me, you won't be afraid forever.

✳ Are you stuck in negativity, doubt, or uncertainty? Exercise your greatest power and freedom—the ability to choose your attitude—and choose an attitude that makes you feel better. Choosing a positive attitude is a no-brainer; it makes you feel better right now. Use some of the techniques from chapter 9 to remind yourself that the Universe is truly on your side.

Okay, then you're right on course for getting answers, the answers that are best for you, from Spirit. Steady on my friend.

It's all coming together beautifully. I know that. And soon enough you'll know it too.

EPILOGUE
The Psychic Comedian

Life takes some surprising turns. For me, at some point between writing this book and getting it to the printer, I made an astonishing discovery about myself: I love to perform stand-up comedy. In writing and performing comedy, I felt I was discovering my own bliss. As a result of this unearthing, *Getting Answers* almost didn't make it to press. For several weeks I was baffled—sitting in that foggy, pre-answer-dawning stage—as to how this all fit together. How was I, (or was I) to publish this book and to move forward with comedy? It took weeks of my mulling this over, finally landing on the right question, getting a good night's sleep, and having a series of "serendipitous" conversations to clarify for me that this all fit together —and perfectly.

It dawned on me that after publishing this book, I didn't have to do the typical author-read-from-her-book appearances. Instead I could show up with my book and give a comedic version of what lies inside its cover. People could still have the manual in book form, but what they would hear from me would (hopefully) have them giggling rather than taking notes. And thus, Aimée Cartier, the psychic comedian was born.

All of this I came to in a natural way by following the process in this book. Time and time again I am delighted to find that asking questions, listening to the messages, and acting on the guidance I receive leads me to discovering more joy—

even more than I'd ever thought possible. Who knew I would love stand-up comedy so much? Certainly not I! But paying attention and acting on my instincts lead me straight there. Life rarely looks exactly how I envisioned it, but when I simply notice the signs and act on them, I see that it's usually more surprising and always better than I could have imagined.

So, if you'd like me to make an appearance at your bookstore, or show up at your conference, with my following-your-intuition comedic version of *Getting Answers,* you can contact me through my website: www.spreadingblessings.com.

Until then, align with the highest good, ask your questions, be patient, receive your answers, and *ACT* on them. In so doing, I'm sure you'll discover what I have: The Universe is just waiting to give you the best ride of a life!

Praise & Thanks

No one person can do anything alone. This book wouldn't have been possible without the help of many people. First and, to my mind, foremost of these is *Getting Answers'* original cheerleader, Mary Kay Rauma. For months Mary Kay and I were the only ones who knew of this book's existence. I can honestly say that without her support and encouragement, this book would not be in your hands today. Thank you so much MK!

To Kirsten Szykitka, *Getting Answers'* first editor, I am so grateful for your corrections, your time, and most of all your friendship. To Margaret Bendet, this book's final editor, I was delighted to work with you again in this way. I relish your expertise, keen observations, efficient pen, and general being. Thank you.

So many people have believed in me and provided me vital support, encouragement, and feedback along the way. I especially want to thank Megan Kupko Hubbs, Neil Harrington, Renée Baribault, Michael Meade, Jacob Lakatua, Rhoda Bolton, Stephen Silha, and Dana Renault for their help—and Tracy Barrett and Jacqui Lown whose artistic talent and expertise made this book all come together in a beautiful package. Then there were those who, while not involved in the specific details of bringing this book into being, continued (and continue) to hold the vision of my success and happiness in their hearts and beings. Cyndee Cartier, Debi Elliot, and Leah Mann come to mind especially.

In short, I feel blessed to be surrounded by so many people—those I've mentioned and some I haven't—who truly love and believe in me.

Though not directly related to the creation of this book, I am also indebted to the wonderful community of friends that I live in and among. Your companionship, songs, poems, imaginations, heartfelt friendship, and authentic beings continue to inspire me day by day. I feel blessed to share this earth with the creative loving people that surround me. Without the sharing of the stories of our everyday lives—including both the laughter and the tears, over the countless glasses of wine and tea—my life would be an empty shell. I love you all so much, and I hope you know that each of you adds beauty to my life.

Last, but certainly not least, I want to offer special thanks to all who supported the publication of this book by donating generously and by buying advance copies of this book so its publication could happen gracefully. Among those Elias Reitz; Jeffrey Slock; Merrilee Runyan; Kelly Hoyt; Jason Culp; Cedric Gagnaire; Joshua Sage; Joe, Richard, and Bruce Cartier; Dana Renault; and Cathy deSmet deserve special thanks. Thanks to all of you; I couldn't have done it without your support!

So much love and so much gratitude!

AIMÉE

CPSIA information can be obtained
at www.ICGtesting.com
Printed in the USA
FSHW021254040419
56968FS